SEEING SPIRITS

OPENING THE EMPATHIC DOOR

Katie Hopkins

KATIE HOPKINS

First Edition:
First printing

PUBLISHED BY HAUNTED ROAD MEDIA, LLC
www.hauntedroadmedia.com

United States of America

KATIE HOPKINS

This book is dedicated to and in the remembrance of:

Donald C. Hass
Delores I. Hopkins
James G. Hopkins
Robert A. Novotny

KATIE HOPKINS

ACKNOWLEDGMENTS

I would have never found my love for the paranormal if it wasn't for my job at the Grout Museum District at the Rensselaer Russell House Museum. I owe a lot to the Russell Family for showing me that life does exist after death.

My husband, Josh. If it wasn't for this field I would have never met the love of my life. He supports me in everything I do. The spirits were definitely leading us to each other that day back in September 2012, when I went to the location he was running.

My family, my Mom and Dad, siblings, brother-in-law, my brother's fiancé, my nephew and my in-laws (Josh's parents and siblings) all accept me for who I am and support my life as a paranormal investigator. They never doubt me and always are encouraging me to do more. My nephew will definitely be an investigator in-training soon.

Also, to Adam D. Tillery, Mike Ricksecker, and Vanessa Hogle for inspiring me to write my experiences and encouraging me to do so. Also, for Adam's participation in this book of his amazing illustrations.

Last, but not least, my friends. They all show excitement and support for me in this field. Also, to the many friends I have made in this field. Thank you for your on-going support.

KATIE HOPKINS

TABLE OF CONTENTS

KATIE HOPKINS

FOREWORD

I've always believed in the afterlife. I have "seen" spirits (I will explain why I put that in quotes a little later), since I was a little girl. The first one I can remember was when our elderly neighbor died and we were over at the house, and I saw him in his rocking chair back and forth in the basement. The chair he was sitting in was one of those old wooden rocking chairs with the spindles for the back. It was pretty old and rickety. He was a pretty hefty guy, thick, never really smiled too much, but he looked as he did when he was living. He was in jeans and a plaid shirt, and his hair was short and combed over to cover the bald spot on the top of his head. He sat there looking straight forward, just rocking back and forth. He also had on an old pair of loafers, almost like slippers.

At the time, I didn't think anything of it. I thought my mind was playing tricks on me. I was only about 10 years old, so I did not really understand what I was seeing, or I thought I was dreaming. The only way I thought there was to communicate with ghosts was through an Ouija Board, which usually made me scream and run out of the room!

I have never told anyone this story before, because back then I didn't know what it meant, and I didn't want to be considered "weird" or "odd" and I didn't want to be told I was lying or making it up. Now I know what I witnessed was real, and people can take it or leave it however they want. In time, almost 13 years later, I would come to understand why I am the way I am.

Once I became a busy pre-teen through my teenage years, the "seeing" of spirits ceased. I was too busy with being a teenager and fitting in. I was active in sports as well, so this, perhaps, is what kept my mind off of things. So, I was not as open when I was younger. They do say that children are more susceptible to spirits than adults, it is because their minds have not been "fixed" on what to believe. They are open and vulnerable. Maybe this is what was happening to me as a child?

Around my senior year of high school is when the "ghost shows" started to become popular. This was the beginning of *Ghost Hunters* and *Ghost Adventures*. I started watching them because it intrigued me. I didn't know if they were real or what I believed, but I thought it was cool that these people got access to some of the most historic buildings in the United States and even international (with the beginning of *Ghost Hunters International*).

This brings me to my love for history. I was more intrigued by the buildings at first than what could still be lurking around in them. I wanted to go witness this history myself. As Jeff Belanger says, "History is just one big ghost story."

Maybe this is why I decided to become a History major in college and graduated with a Bachelor of Arts in History. Perhaps it was the spirits guiding me to this as this would decide my future in the paranormal, as well as my personal future in being guided to my husband.

My paranormal journey began when I was really young, but it would take off in 2012 when I would witness my first paranormal experiences as an adult, and it would bring back many memories I had almost forgotten.

This book is to show you the evolution of my paranormal experiences and how they have changed over the last nearly six years, and even how they are similar to when I was a young girl. If only the paranormal field would have been at its height in the late 1990s, I bet my childhood paranormal experiences would have made a lot more sense to me. I will start off with my first experiences, before my first paranormal investigation, and continue on with the development of me "seeing" spirits. Again, I will explain the quotes when we get to those chapters.

It would not occur to me until about 2013 how much I needed the paranormal field in my life. "Needed" sounds like a strong word, but it has shaped me as a person, both in the field and personally. Again, I give the paranormal field a lot of credit for leading me to the love of my life. You'll hear a story about the first time we met in this book, and the paranormal experiences we had at our first investigation together.

KATIE HOPKINS

THE BEGINNING

In 2009, I took on an internship that I really didn't know if I would like. I was teaching simple machines to third graders at the Bluedorn Science Imaginarium, which is part of the Grout Museum District in Waterloo, Iowa. I was a History Major. I didn't know anything about science, but I wanted to get my "in" with a museum so I could eventually intern in other areas (which included history) or work there in the future. This internship came to an end at the end of the 2010 school year, and I was not given a job since there were no positions open. So, I decided to do an internship that allowed me to travel. I ended up going to Germany for four months and then Hawaii for another four months.

Talk about places where paranormal activity is pretty much a given! I visited Dachau Concentration Camp, Neuschwanstein Castle, Switzerland, Paris, The Louvre, and so much more! I saw the crematorium and the thousands unknown graves of those who had perished during the horrific time of the Holocaust.

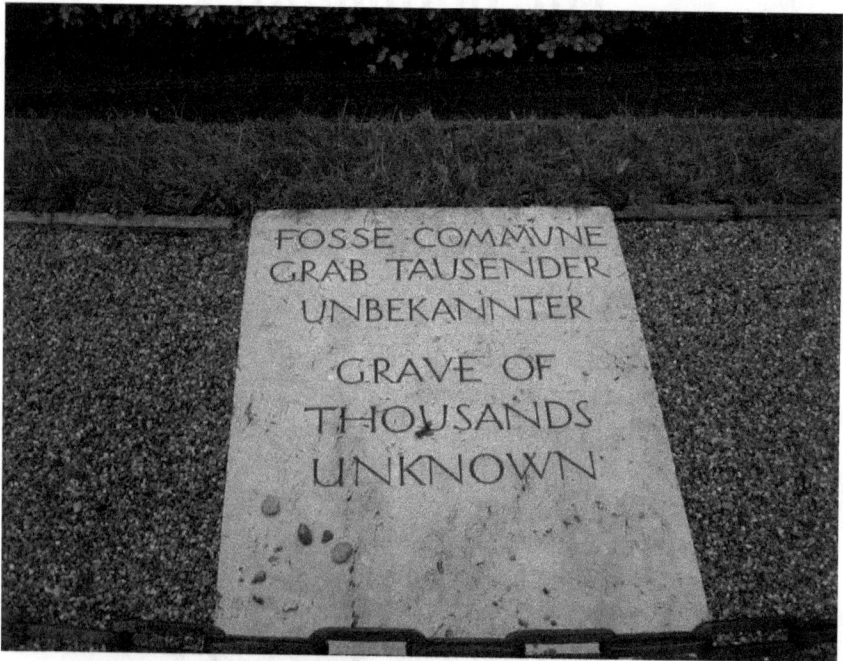

If only my paranormal experiences would have happened before this trip, I bet it would have been much different. I do remember, though, hearing footsteps in our apartment, which dated back before World War II and belonged to the Germans during the war. There were tunnels that we had to walk through in order to get to the laundry room. I never wanted to go by myself. I didn't understand why at the time, I just thought old creepy tunnels, but now I understand. The walls were filled with energy from German soldiers from World War II. One had the feeling of being watched while in the tunnels, and you never wanted to stay down there for a long time. I can look back now and "see" them there, they look confused, wondering why this place has now been invaded with American soldiers.

This also goes for Hawaii. I lived on Pearl Harbor. I visited the site of the *USS Arizona* where you stand over the wreckage. You can feel the energy from the men who went down with the ship. Oil still spews from the ship and makes a shiny gloss over the top of the water. There is also the *USS Utah* which you can still see the wires and part of the ship sticking out of the water. While I was there looking at it, I felt so much sorrow and sadness, it is a very eerie feeling. I never thought that I could possibly be feeling what the men felt that went down with the ship until later on when I learned more about the paranormal. Looking at the pictures still to this day gives me a pit in my stomach.

I could go on and on about my travels, but that would be for another book. It was when I got back from Hawaii that my paranormal journey would recommence from where I left off when I was 10 years old.

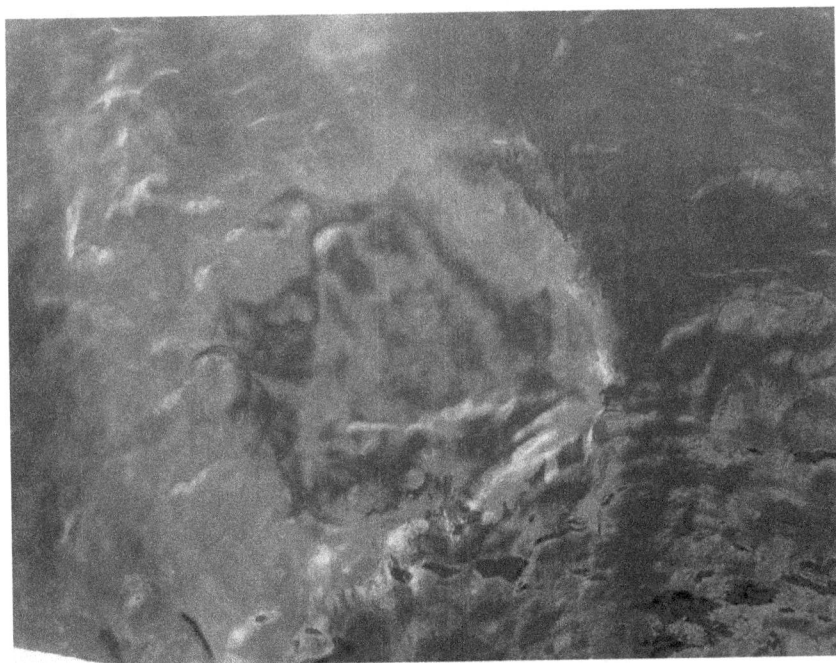

In the Fall of 2011, I took on another internship at the Grout Museum District, but this time, I was teaching an educational program one Saturday a month based upon the television show *Fetch!*. I loved teaching, so I enjoyed this. I wasn't necessarily teaching history, but I did throw in a ghost theme for Halloween! This internship was at the Imaginarium again, however, I became friends with one of the Museum Assistants that worked at the Rensselaer Russell House museum a lot.

I asked her one day, "Is it haunted?"

And, so it begins.

She said that it definitely was haunted. She always felt like she was being watched, she heard footsteps, and even from time-to-time she would hear a voice.

I said, "Okay I have to get in this house and take a tour."

One day before my internship, she took me on a tour of the house. The house takes you back to the late 1800s. It still holds artifacts from the Russell-Lamson families, which adds so much character to the home. It brings the Nineteenth Century back to life when you walk through the front doors. It wasn't until we got upstairs that I would witness something that would make me, one, jump, but two, curious.

I'll start off with a little history. On September 2nd, 1862, Genevieve Russell (daughter of Rensselaer and Caroline Russell, who built the home) fell down a cistern and drowned. She was just shy of her sixth birthday.

In the Nineteenth Century it was common to take post-mortem photographs of your loved ones, especially children. There is a post-mortem photograph of Genevieve Russell in the parent's bedroom. I was looking at this photograph when my friend was explaining some history to me about the room, and all of the sudden I felt a little hand grab the back of my leg on my calf. I couldn't believe it. I grabbed my leg, looked at my friend and told her what happened since she looked at me when I grabbed my leg as if to ask, "What are you doing?"

I smiled when this happened. I told her what I had just experienced, and I was all of the sudden taken back to being 10 years old and knowing that spirits do exist. It's not just the hoopla of the TV shows. So naturally, I had to figure out what was in this house!

I was still an intern at that time, but knew the Director of Historical Programs, who was also pretty much in charge of the house. She eventually would offer me a job as a Museum Assistant a few months after the investigation! I asked her about performing a paranormal investigation at the house, and she said as long as the board was okay with it, it could happen. I put together a presentation on why it would be a good idea, and low and behold the board thought so, too.

It was on February 17th, 2012, that I would acquire the title of "Paranormal Investigator." This would also be the time I would connect with the Russell Family and have an everlasting connection with them, especially Genevieve.

The investigation began, and the house was active from the get-go. There were footsteps, voices, feelings of being watched, even some odd, not-so-happy feelings. My first portion of the investigation began in the parlor with the 1889 Steinway Grand Piano, which belonged to Lillian Russell-Lamson (other daughter of Rensselaer and Caroline). I sat down at the piano, and started to communicate with Genevieve. At this time, I do not use the flashlight as an investigative tool, but back then I was an amateur and I thought it was pretty awesome! Also, we were getting direct responses, and I could just tell it was Genevieve, we also had the K2 Meter setup which was also validating responses. All of this evidence can be seen on the episode of the television *My Ghost Story* that I was on and spoke about this investigation.

As the night progressed, I was in the "control room" while some of the guys investigated. Over the walkie-talkie, one of the investigators asked me what the "Grandpa's name was" I responded with "Richards," and as soon as "Richards" came across the walkie, the piano played one note. Could this be the spirit of William Richards (Caroline's Father) saying, "Yep that's me!" or was it another spirit playing tricks on us?

Richards lived in the home with the family for a while as his wife had passed on and he was elderly. He stayed in the alcove in the back of the house (today it's the office).

Many paranormal occurrences happened that evening. However, this was the kickoff to the reengagement of my paranormal journey. When I became a Museum Assistant, I spent a lot of time in the Russell House by myself. I would hear footsteps, voices, shuffling in the kitchen (my office was right off of the kitchen in the back alcove), and better yet, I could sense when the Russell's were there.

I will never forget my first paranormal investigation, and I'm thankful for this investigation and the Russell Family for, once again, making me open to the paranormal, which has now taken me on many journeys, to many different places.

KATIE HOPKINS

THE SNOWDEN HOUSE

The Snowden House is also part of the Grout Museum District in Waterloo, Iowa. When I became a Museum Assistant around March 2012, I also took on responsibilities to plan events at the Snowden House. I was definitely okay with this! Another potentially haunted house I could run? You bet! The Snowden House is actually very unique. It no longer looks like a home on the inside, but more of an event hall.

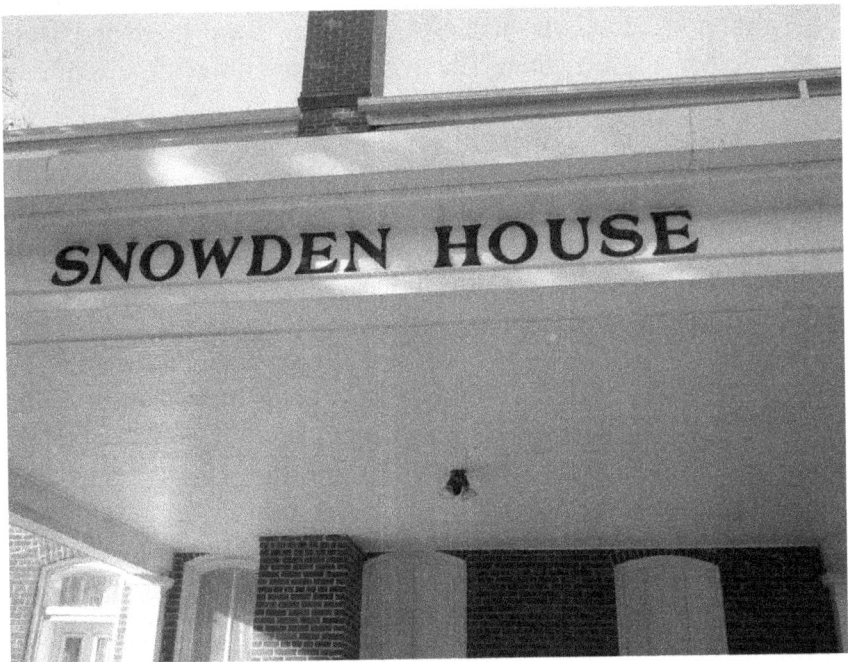

The Snowden House is right next to the Russell House (now in the same "parking lot"). The home was built in 1881 by William Snowden. He purchased the land from Rensselaer Russell. The home was so grand and so large that this was the Snowden's summer home. During the winter months, the home was too difficult to heat due to its size, so the Snowden's would go to Mr. Snowden's pharmacy. The Snowden's did not live in the home very long, since Mr. Snowden died in 1889, leaving his wife Delia sole owner. She transferred the property to Lillian Russell-Lamson, and in September 1922, the Waterloo Women's Club purchased the home.

The interior of the home is now structured from the Women's Club, who renovated the home. The upstairs is now a stage/theater area; there is still a kitchen and dining room. The large room in the front of the home would have been split in two parlor areas when the Snowden's lived there.

I spent a lot of time at the Snowden House while also working at the Russell House. I created events that were held at the Snowden House, and prior to the events, I would prepare the home.

I first noticed activity in the house when I was there preparing for a Mother and Daughter Tea event. I was in the large room on the main floor and upstairs I heard a loud bang and footsteps right after the bang. I ran upstairs to see if anything had fallen over, and nothing was even slightly out of the ordinary, let alone anything that looked like it had fallen that hard to cause that loud of a bang.

I went back downstairs and finished getting the large room ready for the event. As I was walking to the back door to exit the home, I heard another loud bang upstairs and this time a laugh and footsteps. I ran back upstairs, concerned that someone was in the house with me. I wasn't sure how they would have gotten inside since the door was locked, but I was convinced someone was in the house. I looked all around upstairs, behind the stage curtains, and nothing. This had my heart pumping really fast, so I quickly left the home and went back over to the Russell House, one haunted house to the next.

It was almost the end of my shift, so I went to the alcove, wrote down my hours on my time sheet, packed up and went home. My mind kept replaying the events at the Snowden House, which clearly triggered me asking my boss, "Can we investigate the Snowden House?"

She said we could, so I quickly called up my friends who had the paranormal investigation team, and said, "Hey, I have another one for you!"

They quickly jumped on the opportunity and we were investigating the Snowden and Russell Houses in the same night about two weeks later.

The Snowden House we would come to find is very active with paranormal activity. We hadn't even started the investigation, and I was sitting up in the theater area with one of the girls from the team. We were just having casual conversation, sitting in chairs and looking up at the stage. All of the sudden, the back curtain on the stage started to move. We thought it was just a draft or something from the heater.

We were so wrong.

While we continued our conversation, we kept looking at the curtain and discovered what was moving the curtain when we saw a hand poke out from in between the curtain opening! This hand was very large hand and made a grabbing motion when it came out from behind the curtain.

We thought one of our friends was playing a trick on us just to get us worked up, so we jumped up, we went up to the curtain and pulled it open to find... there was no one there. We looked at each other in shock, and then ran downstairs to tell the others what had just happened. They were all intrigued and excited for the investigation.

A few of the other investigators were going to go upstairs to see if they could experience any activity. The stairs that lead upstairs are actually two sets of stairs, one set leading to a landing and the other that leads up to the door that goes into the theater area. One of the investigators reached the landing and then suddenly just sat down. We asked him what was going on, and he said he couldn't move anymore; it was like something had just went through him and took his energy. So, we all gathered on the landing of the stairs and we ALL could feel what he was feeling. There was something so strong on that landing that was taking our energy. In order for spirits to manifest, they need energy, and sometimes human energy is what they decide to utilize in order to give us investigators what we want -- activity. Needless to say, the spirits were very active that evening.

The team that I had reached out to investigate were good friends of mine at the time, so I always would cook a nice meal for us to eat before the investigation. We sat down in the dining room, ate and enjoyed our dinner until the sun went down. We would hear a footstep and a bang here and there while we were eating which only made us more excited to investigate. The sun went down, and it was time to start.

26

The investigation began with half of the group in the Russell House and half of us in the Snowden House. I started in the Snowden House since I was extremely curious to figure out who was in there. We were in the basement area and we were conducting an electronic voice phenomenon (EVP) blast. I asked who was there with us, and when we listened back, we heard someone had answered me! The name that came across the audio recorder was "Anna." After some research, we found out one of the servants of the Snowden's had been named Anna! That was so exciting to find this research, and we wonder if this is the Anna that worked for the Snowden's.

As the investigation continued we were in the theater area. While in the theater area we heard what sounded like a piano playing. There is a beautiful grand piano in the theater area that is still used today for many events. While we thought we were hearing music, all of the sudden one of the investigators and myself felt like the room was filled with people, just as if there was an event going on. However, this event was not a modern event, or one that we would put on today. We felt like the room was filled with people from the 1920s and they were dancing. This experience in my opinion was a residual haunting happening in front of our eyes.

A residual haunting is like a "record player". It is a moment in time, in history that replays in the present day. These spirits do not usually know you're there, they are just living in this moment as they were in history. A residual haunting can occur any minute, hour, day, month, year, etc. It is just like that event has been stamped into the energy at that point in time. This experience lasted for about five minutes. We stayed and were mesmerized by the music and the figures dancing. Once it was done, we went back downstairs and took a quick break. The investigation was very active. This would only make me more curious and intrigued to hold another investigation.

As a Museum Assistant and being in charge of the Russell House, I was part of the Rensselaer Russell House Museum Society. This society creates events and such in order to raise money for the Russell House. These funds are not for operational funds, but for renovations and other upkeep of the home. I wanted to give my all and help raise money for the home since I cared for it so much. The historian in me had a lightbulb light up above my head, and I came up with a fundraiser that turned out to be very successful. I went to the board and told them one thing that people really are intrigued by are customs during the Victorian Era. Another thing people are intrigued by is the afterlife and spirituality. As a historian, I had researched Victorian funeral customs. Victorian funerals are very different than the funerals we have today. This brought me to create a Victorian Funeral Fundraiser Dinner Theater. This would consist of actors, and a set, and artifacts (that were actually from the Victorian Era, which you can see at the end of this chapter). The other thing this would require: more research. I love research! Also, the main funeral that we would highlight would be Genevieve Russell's funeral. Her funeral was held in the Russell Home in the formal parlor. The guests would also enjoy a real Victorian Era meal. I don't remember all of the items on the menu, but I do remember the incredible chocolate cake we had for dessert. I love chocolate.

We had 80 tickets available for this event. I did not expect for it to sell out, but I hoped for a good crowd. A few days before the event, I got an email telling me the fundraiser has sold out! I was so excited, so nervous and so ready. I was nervous since I wanted all of the guests to enjoy the event, and I was excited because I was so in my element. We had amazing donors donate items from funeral homes to display so guests could walk through a gallery of artifacts and photographs before the actual event. The event was held in the theater area at the Snowden House. Now the paranormal investigator side of me was starting to click. My question I kept asking myself, "Will this spark more activity in the house?" It sure did!

About a month after the fundraiser, my friends came back again to investigate. Activity was at its highest! We experienced cold spots, and again, the energy "stealing" spots. The EVPs we caught were the best EVPs I had heard in a long time, if ever. When I first started in the field, I was quick to listen to audio. I would get home at 5:00am and *have* to listen to my audio recorder. After the investigation, I got home, laid in bed, and started to listen.

The first EVP I came across was from the large room in the front of the Snowden House. It was a woman coming across saying

"Not this house!" What was she referring to? "Not this house!" I did not get it at all. To this day, I still do not know what she was referring to. Was it one of the women from the Waterloo Women's Club? Was it one of the Snowden's? I am open to suggestions and ideas of what she may have been referring to. This voice was so loud and so distinct. I can still hear it in my head when I think of it. This wouldn't be the only EVP to make me sit up in my bed though that night.

I kept listening and the next EVP I came across was from up in the theater area. This next voice was a little more disturbing, not in a scary way, but a sad way. The voice was a child and it said, "Mommy." I was very confused by this EVP. Was this Genevieve coming over from the Russell House, or was this a completely different child? I do not think it was another spirit "posing" as a child. I really, genuinely believe this was a child spirit looking for their mother. I do not know if this spirit ever did find their mother, or whomever they were looking for, but I hope they are at peace.

The next EVP had the same voice as the, "Not this house," spirit. In this EVP, the spirit sounded like they were clenching their teeth together in anger. This was caught in the large room on the main floor. The EVP said, "We heard it from below." What? What in the world does this mean? What do they mean by "below"? Again, I still do not know the context of this EVP or whom this is saying it. Answers still remain to be found when it comes to these EVPs that were caught in 2012.

After the first few investigations, the home became a little bit darker and a little bit heavier. There were times I would need to go over to the home to get some work done, and I couldn't even go into the house. I would turn around, go back to the Russell House and say, "I'll do it tomorrow."

I have always wondered who was haunting the Snowden House. My thoughts are that many of the spirits are passersby. Also, with a nursing home right next to the house, those spirits there could very well make their way over to the beautiful home. Not to mention, the second investigation we had, there was an ambulance at the nursing home. Could that have sparked activity? There are still many questions to be answered about the Snowden House spirits.

Victorian Funeral Fundraiser Photographs:

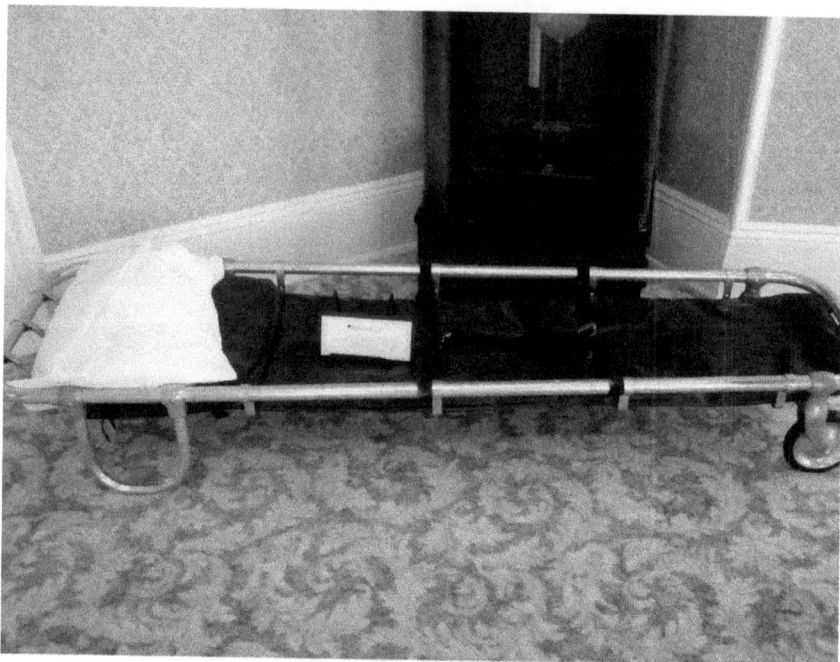

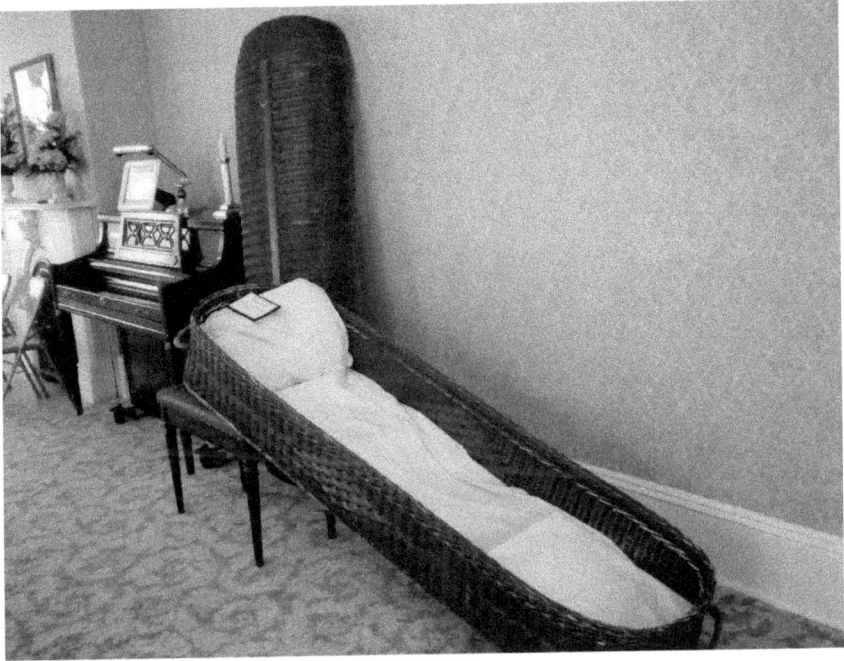

KATIE HOPKINS

DANIEL ARTHUR'S

I came across Daniel Arthur's restaurant when I was with the 319 Paranormal team. Even though I'm a long resident of the Cedar Rapids area, I will be honest. I didn't know about the restaurant until I went there for a paranormal investigation. This actually came as a surprise to me due to the history of the home. You'd think a historian like me would be all over this house and researching it from top to bottom. How this slipped through the cracks is beyond me.

The home was built in 1870 and was part of "Mansion Hill" in Cedar Rapids, Iowa. There were originally six homes that were part of "Mansion Hill", and this home is one of the only still standing, with the exception of a very popular mansion in Cedar Rapids called Brucemore Mansion. This is also one of the oldest homes that was part of "Mansion Hill". The home was built by Maria Carpenter, who was a widow of prominent businessman Gabriel Carpenter. The house was used by multiple families up until 1920 when it was created into the Beatty Funeral Home. It was the funeral home for the next 60 years until 1980, and then became a restaurant. The original embalming sink is still in the basement. The upper floors, which were the bedrooms when it was a home, was used to store caskets. You can still see the "staging" area where the caskets were displayed during visitations. There are even some of the Funeral Director's belongings in the basement, which include a desk and a safe.

Numerous ghost stories have come from this building. Many of the restaurant workers at Daniel Arthur's, which has since closed in 2014, talked about kitchen utensils, silverware, glasses and plates being thrown. They even said that some of the freshly wrapped silverware on a table was suddenly unwrapped within a five-minute time frame. The employee wrapped the silverware and left it on the table. They then went into the kitchen, when they came back the silverware had been unwrapped and spread all over the table. I was so excited to get into this home. It is definitely a "hidden gem" of Cedar Rapids.

The only two investigations I conducted at Daniel Arthur's were actually public events that the 319 Paranormal team held. I was okay with this, though, as a lot of the time there is so much energy from the guests that a lot of activity happens.

We started off with a group session in the "Viewing Room". This is where a majority of the tables are setup now for the restaurant, but when it was a funeral home, this is where the caskets were viewed. We started off with a ghost box session, where we got the typical "get out" and "hello" responses. I was ready to venture off from the large group and investigate with a smaller group to see what kind of activity we could get.

A small group and I went upstairs to one of the bathrooms. This would have been the master bathroom which is off of the master bedroom. We sat on the floor and were just listening to see if we could hear anything. There is a door in the bathroom that is just across from the entry way. You walk in, to the left is a gorgeous large bathtub, and to the right there is a sink, toilet and another shower. Then right in front of you is another door. I went to go open this door and found out it was locked. I knocked on the door, not thinking I would get any type of response. When I knocked again, a knock came from the other side of the door. We were in disbelief. Did this really just happen? So, I knocked again and said, "Hello."

A few seconds later, there was another knock! Just so we could make sure there was nothing on the other side of this door, we went and asked the owners what was behind the door. They said it was nothing but a storage area, they were the only ones with a key and the only way to get in there is through that door in the bathroom. All right!

We went back up to the bathroom and started to investigate again. I again knocked, but there were no more knocks. We did hear shuffling on the other side of the door, though, as if the person on the other side was wearing a large silky dress. It sounded like the person was twirling, so the dress just kept making a shuffling noise. We then got the K2 out, and while there were no readings within the bathroom, the minute we took it to the door, it went all the way up to red! I really wish I could go back there and investigate again to get more answers from whatever is on the other side of that door.

After this session in the bathroom, we headed downstairs. This is where the restaurant kept their kitchen supplies and also dry and canned ingredients. Walking by the embalming sink always gives you a very uneasy feeling. This could be just because of what it is. We didn't investigate around it. We went back to a little room off of the large room with the embalming sink. This room is right across from the office area of the Funeral Director.

The owners had given us a name of a spirit with which they have had multiple encounters. They gave this spirit the name Buddy. They think Buddy is a four-year old boy. There is no history to validate this spirit, but we went with this and tried to communicate with Buddy. We used the K2 and a mag light to communicate with him. He used both. He did say he was a four-year old boy, he liked it when people visited him, and he likes to stay in the basement. We were having a great conversation with Buddy, and then all of the sudden, the communication stopped. It was just like Buddy had left us altogether. One of the event guests asked if he was being held back from speaking to us, and the light turned on. We do not know what was holding him back or who it was, but Buddy did not speak with us the rest of the night.

When we finished our investigation, we conducted evidence review the next day. I couldn't wait to listen to the audio from the bathroom and the basement since we were having so many great personal experiences. In the bathroom audio, you could hear the knocks and you could hear the shuffling. When we were about to leave the bathroom, on the audio we heard a woman say, "Don't leave!"

We could have stayed and listened to her more. I am still curious as to what she wanted to tell us. Was this woman stuck behind the bathroom door? I continued to listen, and that was the only voice we caught on audio from the bathroom.

Then I listened to the basement audio. We did catch a child laughing and saying, "Play with me." I still do not know if this is actually a child or if it is another spirit disguising itself as a child. It was a little creepy listening back to it. Then there were some other noises, which one sounded like a growl and one sounded like a grunt. That was about all of the audio we actually caught.

Our personal experiences were definitely the highlight of this investigation. One of our guests even reported back to us that they saw a shadow figure at the bottom of the stairs that lead from the second floor to the entrance of the restaurant.

I still have questions and long for answers on who is haunting the old Daniel Arthur's restaurant. I wonder if Maria Carpenter is the one behind the bathroom door. Is she stuck here? Who is Buddy? I wonder if my questions will ever be answered.

HEIGHTENED SENSITIVITY AT FARRAR SCHOOL

Months had passed since my first investigation at the Russell House. One of the locations that I had longed to go to was the Farrar School. I was not part of a paranormal team when I first started off, so I was finding events to attend that I could get to these locations I wanted to go to.

I came across a team called 319 Paranormal. They were hosting an event at the Farrar School in June 2012, plus, one of my favorite Hawkeye Alumni Football Players, Tim Dwight, would be attending this event too, so I HAD to go! They were holding a contest on their page that if you had the most referrals to their page you got a free ticket to the event. So, I got on Facebook and begged and pleaded with my Facebook friends to like their page so I could go to this event! I won! I had been acquainted with 319 Paranormal from the investigation at the Russel House, and they added me to their team before the event. So, I went to the event at the Farrar School as a team member!

The night of the event was here, I was ready, and I walked into the Farrar School and just felt the rush of excitement like a ton of bricks hitting me. My anxiety level was off the charts, I was so excited. I had finally made it to the Farrar School!

The night began with a group session up in the auditorium area. This area would become one of the most frightening places to me in the next few months. I'll get to that story, shortly. At first, it was pretty quiet, we were getting spirit box hits here and there, but nothing extravagant…. yet.

We decided to split the group up into small groups. One of my teammates, Tim Dwight and I went into the Janitor's Closet which is in one of the staircase landings leading from the first floor to the second floor. This area was never open to the public, but that evening the owners allowed it to be open for our event since this seemed to be a very active area of the building. One of the claims is that the janitor, who has been noted to not be a very nice man, is still roaming in the school. There were allegations against him, which I will not go into, but let's just say in his human state, you wouldn't want to be around him.

We went into the closet and started to investigate. It was just like a burst of negative energy hit me when I was standing in there, I was clenching my fist so hard and standing next to me was Tim Dwight. Remind you, he is one of my favorite Hawkeye Alumni Football players, the last thing I want to do to this man is hit him, but in the state I was in, in that closet, I wanted to hit him so hard. I clenched my fist, took some deep breaths and finally said I needed to get out of there.

We got out of the closet, I took a break and recollected myself, and went onto investigating elsewhere. I did not return to the Janitor's Closet that night, and wouldn't until October 2012 when I was interviewed about my experience for a YouTube paranormal show.

This was not the end to my experiences with the Janitor's Closet, however. The janitor stuck around with me for months after this investigation. My family noticed changes in me, and they weren't good changes. I was angry all of the time, when I am usually a very happy person. I would get mad at the smallest things, and rarely smile.

My family took matters into their own hands and sent me to get Angelic Reiki Healing. This was the best thing they could have ever done for me. I went and the first thing that the Reiki Master said to me was, "Were you in some kind of closet at that school?"

I didn't tell her about the school nor did I tell her about the closet. I think my eyes probably got as wide as they ever could, and I answered with a shaken voice, "Yes."

She then proceeded to tell me that the man that was in that closet had latched himself onto me, and he was the reason for my "moods." She said he saw compassion in me, and that even though he wasn't the nicest man, I still cared for him and wanted to know his story. Thankfully, I was able to rid of his energy and I became myself again. However, this would be the first of many unwanted happenings at the Farrar School.

I went back to Farrar a few months later for the first Iowa ParaCon. I seemed to have been able to kick the janitor and didn't have any experiences with him that night. This would be the night though that I met the wonderful team the C.R.E.E.P.Z. Ghost Commandos (CGC).

I met brothers Adam and Alec Tillery up in the auditorium. My friend and I walked in, and in the corner, Adam was sitting in a chair and Alec standing next to him. They knew we didn't see them since the room was pitch black. So, this was their opportune moment to give us a good scare! I can't remember exactly what Adam did; I think maybe just said, "Hello." But it sure made us jump!

Adam and Alec are now great friends of my husband and I, and I can easily say they are some of the best investigators with which we have ever worked. There will be some stories about our crazy experiences with them later in this book.

For now, I want to go back to where I said the auditorium was the most frightening area for me. Let's fast forward to October 2012, we are back at the Farrar School and I am now with a different team. This was just a regular investigation with just a few teams there. This experience happened fairly early on in the investigation. There were a few people sitting on the stage, and most of us were in a circle on the floor. I started to feel uncomfortable but kept that to myself. I didn't want to be the "scared" one.

Time passed, and the more time passed, the more uncomfortable I got. All of the sudden, I broke into tears and had to leave the room. This was due to the "Crazy Man". To this day, I do not know exactly who he is or what he is. The one thing I can say about him is he has a crooked smile, and looks like how I described him, crazy. He, until about July 2015, had one of the darkest, nastiest energies I had ever encountered. Thankfully, I have not run into him again since this incident, and I hope no one ever does. I think that if I would have been a more veteran investigator, I would have been able to handle him better, but with being in the field for only about 8 months at that time, I was not ready for him.

I have gone back to the Farrar School many times since this encounter with the "Crazy Man," and all have been a lot lighter! There is one room on the third floor, however, that does have a darkness too it, that makes you unable to go into the center of the room. We recently went there with the C.R.E.E.P.Z Ghost Commandos and we all felt a rush of energy in this room. We also had some interesting happenings with the magnetic arrow that the CGC used, one of their tools to try and guide the spirits. The arrow had been setup all night with no disturbances, and when we walked out of the "dark room," all of the sudden the magnet flew off of the tripod and flipped around. We were also there in May 2016 (before the investigation with CGC), and the same feeling in that room occurred for all of us.

I thank the Farrar School and the spirits there for opening me up even more to this field. The "Crazy Man" experience would be the first of many empathic experiences I would have. My knowledge on these empathic abilities has grown, too, and I can now sense more spirit and "see" more spirit. Again, we will get to the quotations around "see" in just a few more stories.

KATIE HOPKINS

STORIES OF EDINBURGH MANOR

September 22, 2012, would change my life forever. I love that I can attribute this to the paranormal field and how it brought me to Josh, my husband. Josh just so happened to be the tour guide at Edinburgh Manor the first night I ever investigated there. It was not even planned for me to be there until about a week and a half before the investigation. The team I met at Iowa ParaCon in July, invited me on their investigation, basically for a "try-out" to be on their team. I took them up on their offer and headed out to Scotch Grove, Iowa, to investigate the infamous Edinburgh Manor.

I remember getting out of my car, walking up to the doors, and felt stupid because I was told to sign a waiver before coming, and I forgot mine at home. So, I walked in, and said, "Hello," and around the corner came Josh. Of course, he had to be cute, so this made asking for a waiver even worse. I asked him for a waiver, and he told me just to sign someone else's. All right, easy enough.

He gave us the tour, told us where the hot spots were, and we began our investigation at dusk. I was excited, because Josh stayed to investigate. I was shy around men, so I just acted friendly and moved on, didn't want him to know I thought he was cute. I stuck with him most of the night, except for when another female investigator and I went into what is called the "Rape Room" and we laid on beds in there. This room is given the name "Rape Room" because a Medium in London did a remote view and said that she could see a woman being raped in there by three men. They were all patients of the Manor. There is no time frame on when this happened, and this is all allegation since this has never been proven with written documentation. However, many incidents like this could have been kept secret, especially in the early 1900s. That is not a story I would like to get into and I hope that if this is a true story that the spirit of that woman can be free and not suffer.

While the other investigator and I lay there, the room started to get darker and darker. We both started to feel our feet being played with, almost like they were tingling and being tickled. Then all of the sudden I felt ice cold over me. I was being held down in the bed, I couldn't move and I was struggling to sit up. I told the other investigator I couldn't move and she no longer felt the sensation on her feet. She got up and asked me if I was okay. I then yelled "GET OFF ME!" and the cold spot went away. I was finally able to get up.

I did not return to that room the rest of the night. We even caught an EVP in that room that says "Look her over" in a male whispery voice.

This was the start to many experiences I would have at Edinburgh Manor.

In April 2013, Josh and I reconnected. I, of course, added him on Facebook after the investigation at the Manor, but we didn't talk much through there. He did message me, though, about a new building his uncle had purchased and that he'd like help researching it since he knew I had a degree in History. Of course, I said, "Yes," but that research would come much later. The night of a paranormal event would bring Josh and I closer together.

There were some great EVPs caught that evening, and even some incredible ghost box. The special guests at the event would also never forget their experiences, as one of them felt like he was slapped across the face and scratched on his back. This would be the night though that would end my time with the team that took me there in September, and I am so thankful for this night that brought me closer to Josh.

Time had passed. Josh was heading out to the Manor and invited me to go with him and his family. I accepted his offer, and we went and investigated. I got to know Josh quite well and we became best friends, eventually creating our own team, Unknown Darkness, in October 2013, which we still have today.

Josh and I, after multiple investigations with him and his family, decided to go out to the Manor on our own. We ended up doing this quite often as we found we got a lot of activity when it was just the two of us. We would even go in -20-degree weather because that is when no one had the Manor booked.

One night, we went and we were investigating the second floor, where "that room" is. Josh and I were just having casual conversation when all of the sudden, the board that was propping the room's door open went flying across the floor, slamming the door shut. We jumped and ran for the rear emergency exit door. We stopped in the room that is down the hall across from "that room" and remembered the keys were in the "safe room" on the first floor, so if we were to exit, we wouldn't be able to get back in. The minute we stopped, we heard loud banging footsteps above us. The craziest part about that is, the attic was above us which is nothing but a bunch of insulation and wooden beams. The vibrations and loudness of these footsteps made it sound like there was an elephant in the attic stomping as hard as it could. Nothing, I mean NOTHING could make that noise if they tried, again only an elephant, and I don't think the owners keep too many elephants in the attic.

We had a long walk down to the main floor to get the car keys and the building keys. We got them, ran out the door to the car and sat there and laughed at what just happened. We tried to soak it in as well, because that was the craziest thing we had experienced ever (at that point in time). This didn't keep us away, though. We went on to investigate the Manor hundreds, if not thousands of times. The next entity we would encounter there would stick with us, even when we weren't at the Manor.

Many people have now heard of "The Joker" since he was the highlight of the *Ghost Adventures* episode that was filmed at Edinburgh Manor. Our experiences go way back with the one to which we gave the name The Joker. The Joker's presence is so well known to us we can always tell when he's around. We get goosebumps, the air is thick and heavy, it's dark, and we can sense his malicious personality.

Josh first came across the Joker when he described him as a spirit who has a, "Joker-like smile." This is how he became The Joker. It's almost as if The Joker knew us so well, that he would always make his presence known to us. He followed us around like a puppy, but a really dark, not-so-nice puppy. The craziest part about him is he doesn't just stay at the Manor.

Josh, a friend of ours and I went to Lexington, Kentucky, in September 2013. On our way home, we stopped at the extremely haunted Bobby Mackey's and did a ghost box session in the parking lot. We asked what their purpose was and a male voice came across and said, "Edinburgh." We instantly knew who was with us. And why wouldn't he go to Bobby Mackey's? It's one of America's most haunted locations, with spirits he probably really likes!

He has also followed us to other locations where we can pick up on his energy. We know his energy, we know when he's around and he likes to surprise us from time-to-time. We also have a ghost box clip of The Joker coming across it, clear as day. I don't know what it is with him, why he follows us. Maybe it's because of the obsession we had with him when we first encountered him; we always wanted him around so we would have a paranormal experience. I think he is the reason for most of the experiences people have at the Manor, and why some spirits do not come out on certain nights. He overshadows them and controls them. Will we ever get rid of The Joker? Probably not.

The last story of the Manor that again shows the traits of being an empath are from April 2014. Josh and I, along with our teammates at the time, were holding an event at the Manor. The

CGC was joining us for this event, as well, as our special guests. When we combine forces with the CGC we usually have some pretty incredible experiences. Usually lights go out, TVs go off (you'll hear about these experiences in the Belvoir Winery Chapter), and in this specific situation at the Manor, there was a crazy thunderstorm coming through. We even told guests if they did not feel comfortable staying for the event, they could leave. There were tornado warnings everywhere, hail was in the forecast, and lots and lots of rain. Our guests were troopers and stuck out the storm. Many do say that storms can heighten activity. I think it gave the spirits extra strength that evening, making their emotions crawl on everyone.

One of my teammates and I started off the night in the basement back by the old padded room. The ceiling in the room is still what I call "crated". You can see a picture of the padded room in the photos from the Manor that is at the end of this chapter. We started the investigation, and right off the bat it was dark and heavy. It was one of those situations where all eyes were on us and, for me, it was all energy was on me.

If you know me, I am not one to just break down and start crying. It takes a lot to get me to cry. For some reason in this situation, I could not dry my eyes. I felt so much sadness and so much pain that I just broke into tears. It was hard to catch my breath. I told my teammate that I needed a break and I went outside. It is definitely against our protocol to leave a room without someone, especially in Edinburgh Manor. However, at this point in time I could have cared less. I was not myself, and I had to get out of there.

The minute I got outside, I was fine. I was still trying to catch my breath, but the tears stopped. I smiled, laughed a little, said, "I have no idea what is going on. Why in the world am I crying so much?"

Mind you, this is before I really knew about being an empath. I knew that spirits could control your emotions at times, but this was way over my head at this point in time, and I didn't realize how much empathic ability I had. So, I turned around went back into the basement. I figured I had shaken off whatever it was that was causing me to become so emotional. The minute I got back down by the padded room, the water works turned back on.

I once again told my teammate I had to go, so I went outside and this time it didn't leave me right away. I had to take deep breaths and find myself again. My teammate was really worried, so he went down to tell Josh and our other teammate at the time that we needed to stop the investigation, to go check on me. I don't remember much before they got outside. I just remember walking around in the front lawn trying to catch my breath and get rid of the tears.

The next thing I remember is Josh standing next to me asking me what was going on. Josh and I had only been dating for a few weeks at this point in time, so I felt like an idiot sitting there bawling my eyes out. I just kept assuring him that I had no idea why I was crying. He consoled me and made me laugh with our little quirky things we still do to this day, and we moved on. However, he told me to not go back in the basement. I listened to him since this night was for our guests at the event. They were there to have a good time and, hopefully, catch some paranormal activity with whatever equipment they may be using or just have personal experiences.

So, I spent the rest of the evening with Adam and Alec from the CGC up on the main and second floors. We still had plenty of activity, lots of bangs and personal experiences. One of our current teammates, Sarah, who went to this event, had "that room's" door hit her in the rear end. That made her jump so high, and is still an experience she talks about today.

Photographs I have taken over the years at Edinburgh Manor:

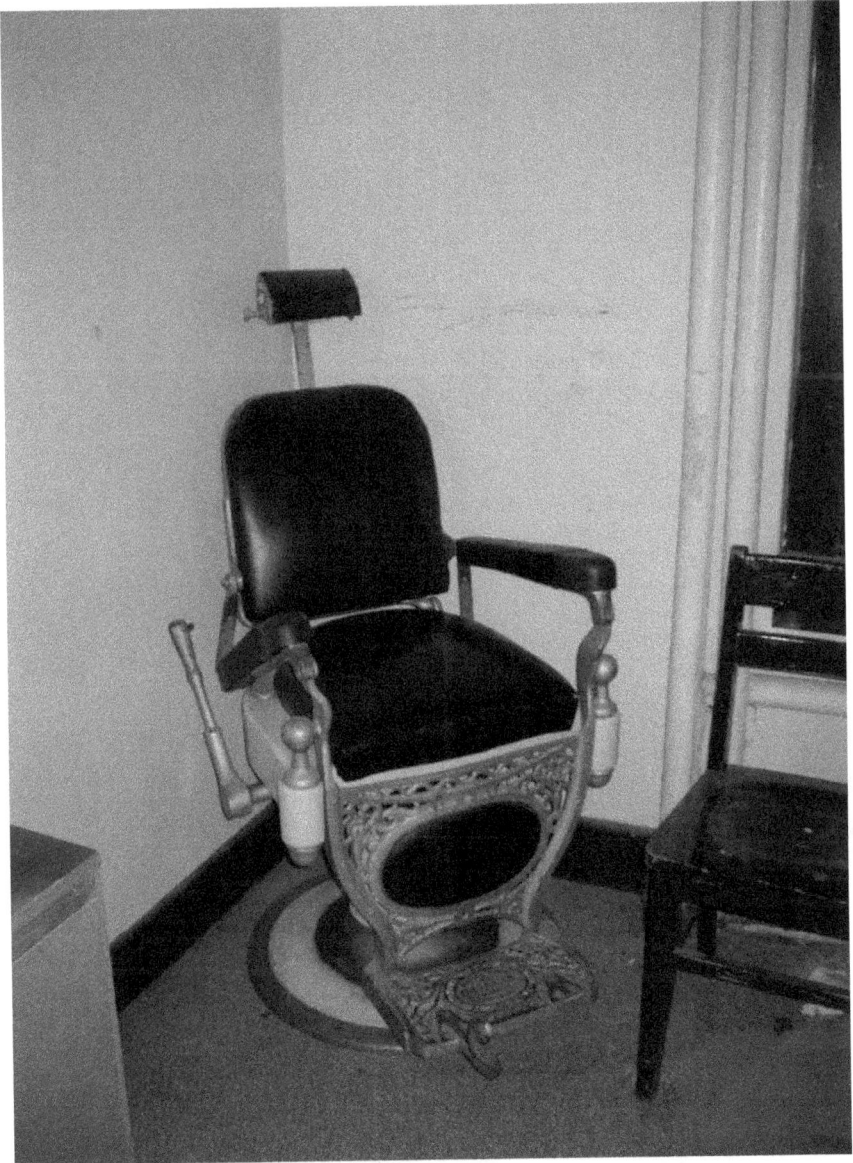

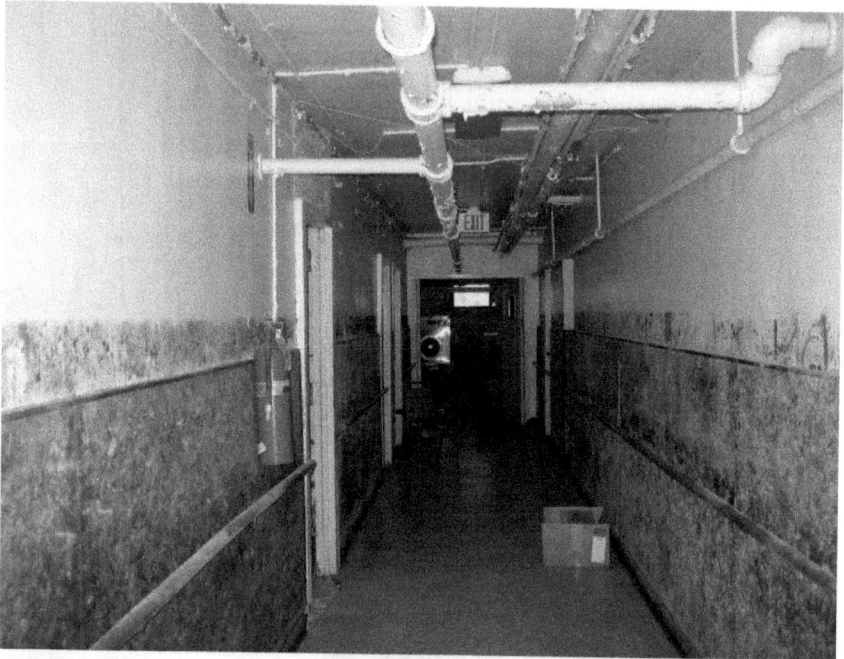

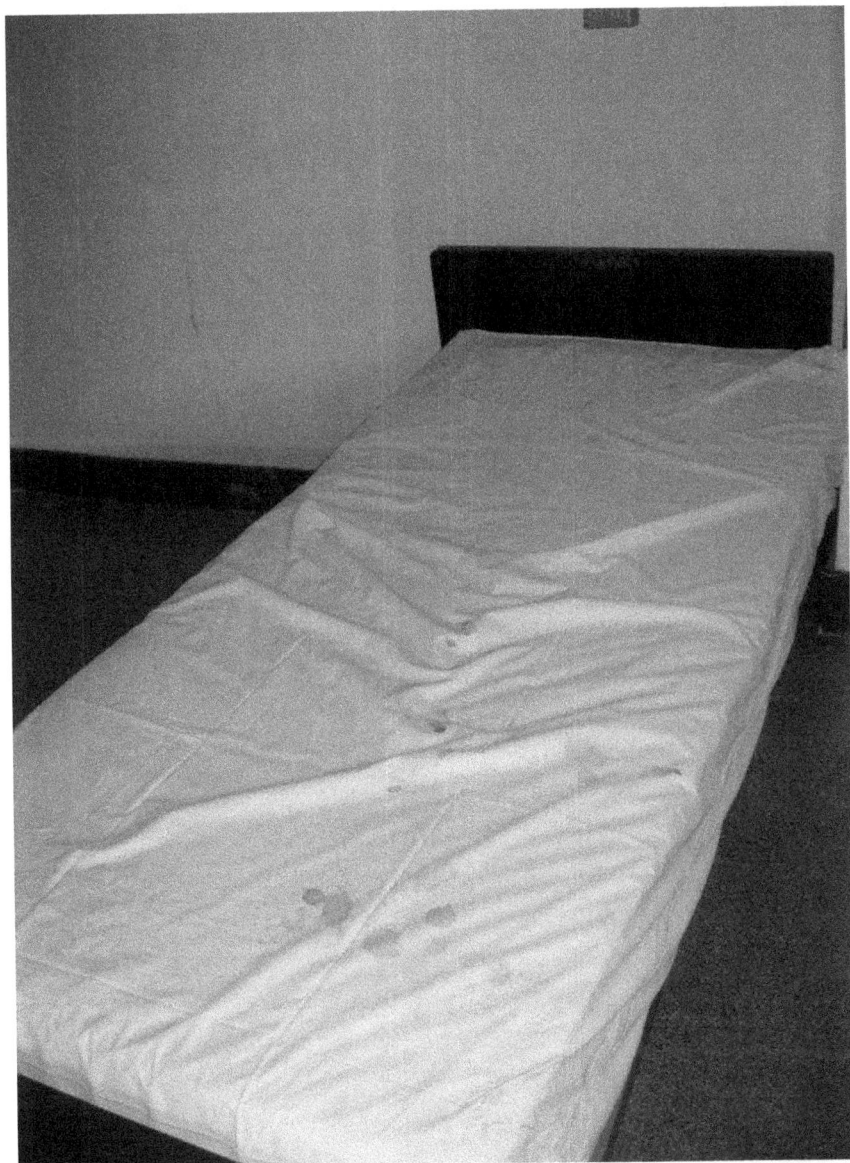

Old Padded Room

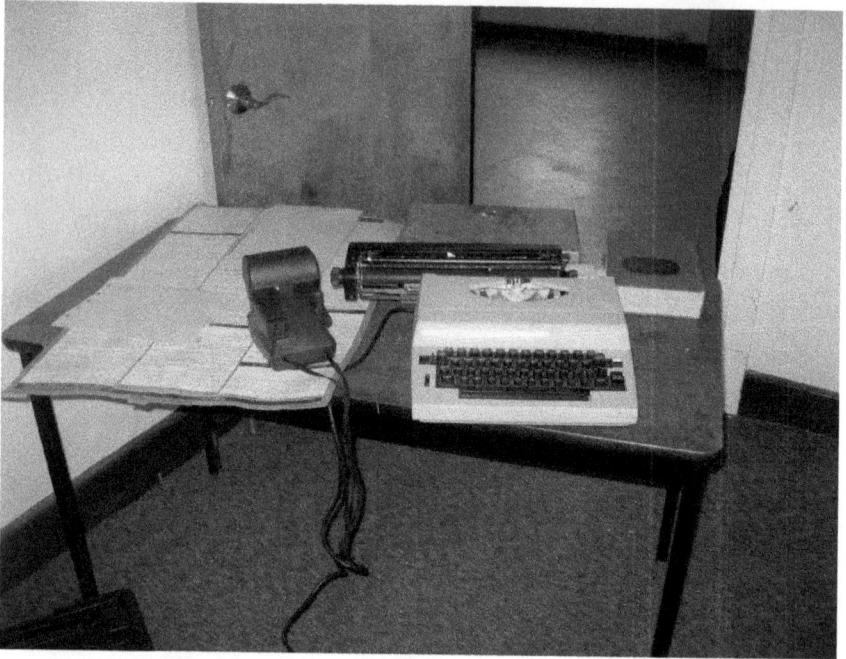

CEDAR FALLS HISTORICAL SOCIETY

I started working at the Cedar Falls Historical Society as the Volunteer and Membership Services Coordinator in October 2012. I found this to be a great opportunity to get some more museum experience and learn more about the operational side of museums. This also gave me the opportunity to do some programming for the museum. Of course, my programming was going to be focused around the paranormal. Luckily, the Executive Director was very open to this and allowed me to start working on some programs. I asked her if she ever had any experiences in the home and she said she had heard some footsteps before, but nothing that scared her.

Just to be clear, it doesn't have to be scary to be paranormal. I've had many experiences that were paranormal and they are not scary. Actually, a majority of my experiences that are paranormal are not scary.

I asked the Executive Director if she would be okay with me conducting a paranormal investigation at the home so I could use that evidence (if we caught any) in the programming I was creating. She was okay with it since she trusted me to not let anything happen to the museum and the artifacts.

I want to first dive into the experiences I had before the investigation. I would often times be in the museum alone. The museum is an old Victorian Home and Carriage House. The portion where my office was located, was the old carriage house. There were many times I would hear things upstairs in the

Victorian home. Whether it be footsteps or whether it be voices, it didn't matter, I heard them ALL THE TIME.

I told some of the other employees at the museum about this, and they said, "Oh, you're just hearing things; this place isn't haunted."

I just ignored them and moved on because I know what I had been hearing. There was one bang that was so loud upstairs it made me run up there to see who was up there. I thought that one of my co-workers had been up there working, but when I got up there, there was no one. There was one area in the museum I usually avoided, and that was the basement. The basement had an old Victorian wooden coffin in it that spewed so much energy, it hit me like a ton of bricks every time I went down there. I do not know what the coffin was actually used for, or if anyone was ever in it, but it was very unsettling looking at it. The basement just had your typical scary basement vibe.

The most memorable experience I had, though, while working there was when I was expecting a volunteer to show up. I was in the back office, and I heard the front door open. The front door had a very distinctive sound to it when it opened, it creaked a little and you could hear the air flow through, like a "whoosh" sound when it was opened. I heard this noise, so I ran to the front to greet the volunteer. To my surprise, the door was still closed and locked, and there was no one in the building. I quickly ran into the parlor area of the Victorian home to see if maybe the volunteer snuck into there. They hadn't. Then I realized, they would have had to have opened the door, locked the door back up and then went somewhere, where I couldn't see them. They wouldn't have had time to do all of that with how quickly I got up and went to the front door. This had my heart racing. I was the only one in the building (that I could see).

The investigation couldn't get there quick enough. Finally, in January 2013 the investigation was conducted. We caught so many EVPs of adults, children and even animals! The investigation began up in the Servant's room on the second floor of the Victorian Home.

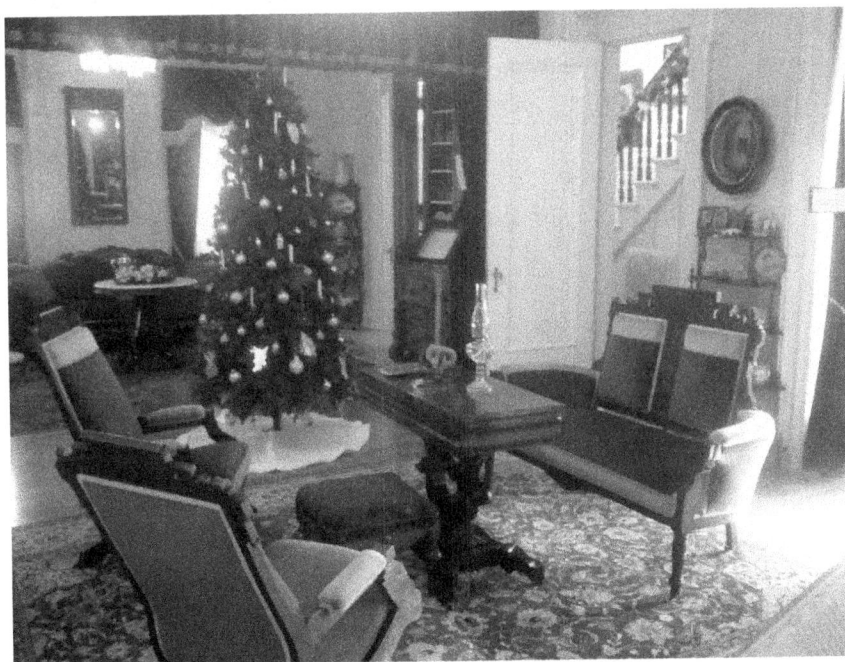

The Servants' room had a very interesting feeling to it. It had a sense of happiness, but then a minute later it would have the feeling of extreme regret. I do not know what the regret meant. In the Servants' room there is also a crib. The servants that worked there did have children and their children would stay in the same room as the mother and father. I still long to know what the regret feeling meant. We did catch some EVPs in this room, but nothing that was clear. There were also some groans and clicks on the audio recorder. What these clicks were, I have no idea.

After we were done in the Servants' room, we went over to the Carriage House Museum, which is connected to the Victorian Home, and went up to the written archives/library room. The written archives/library room would prove to be very active. It was like a game of cat and mouse with this spirit. I would see a little part of him sticking out from behind one of the shelves, and then he'd move really quickly. I say "he" and "him" because you could feel his energy. You could feel a male presence in that room.

I was running around the shelving in the written archives/library room, chasing him around. It felt like a fun game of hide and seek. I would run to the right, see just a portion of his body, like his hand or foot. Then he would run the other way. I thought at this point, I was entertaining a young spirit. The energy was playful and light, and I was having a blast! Until, I saw his entire body.

I turned the back corner to the left -- the shelving in this room is very tall and goes all the way from the floor to the ceiling. I turned the corner and there he was, his full figure. He was a shadow person, but he was not the little boy I thought I was chasing around. He was about seven-and-a-half feet tall and extremely thin. He made me stop in my tracks, and I quickly turned my flashlight on and he disappeared.

Who or what was I just chasing around? I know it was not a child, as I have never seen a seven-and-a-half-foot child. Was this an adult spirit who maybe thought they were a child? I had no clue, but the minute I saw him I became frightened and the energy shifted from happy and light to dark and chilling. This wouldn't be the only time I come across a very tall dark spirit either.

I left the written archives/library and went down to the main area in the Carriage House Museum so I could take a break and recollect my thoughts. What would have happened if I would have stayed in that room longer with that spirit? I didn't know after seeing his full figure if he was "good" or "bad". I am not sure I wanted to find out.

This incident kept me from going up to that room at night, or when it was dark, or even when I was there alone. I didn't want to run into this guy again. Thankfully, my position didn't require for me to go to that room very often, but when I was doing research for events, I would on occasion, need to go in there. The Education Coordinator had a desk near the written archives, so I would go in there when she was up there. This is how bad this incident frightened me.

We then had to do it, we had to go to the basement. It was difficult for me to go down the stairs to the basement. I already had my scare for the night in the written archives/library, I didn't think I needed another one. I did it, though, and I went to the basement. The first thing we did was use the K2 and we put it near the old coffin. At first the readings were low, there was no electromagnetic field detected. After conducting a few communication sessions with the audio recorder and ghost box, the energy started to surround us. It is hard to describe this energy. It was a "confused" energy.

We took the K2 over near the coffin and it went right up to red. We asked a few things about it, and if anyone was attached to it. The light went up to red. We were getting the sense that maybe the spirit that had possibly been in this coffin had some type of abdominal issue. Whether it be they were shot in the stomach or whether it be that they died due to some type of complications with their stomach, we weren't sure. However, my stomach kept getting shooting pains in it.

I look back now and know this could have been an empathic experience. Was I feeling what this person felt? When the coffin was given to the historical society, no information was given with it. The coffin will probably remain a mystery forever.

We concluded the investigation after being in the basement since we were all so tired from our energy being used by the spirits that evening. This would be the only investigation of the Victorian Home and Carriage House Museum at the Cedar Falls Historical Society. Nevertheless, this would not be the end of paranormal activity in the home.

A few days after the investigation I got to the home very early in the morning, and I had been the last one to leave the night before. I parked across the street from the museum and looked up into one of the windows that would have been the master bedroom. The light was on! I made sure every night before leaving that all of the lights were shut off. I text messaged the Executive Director and asked her if anyone had been in the house later the previous night or early that morning. She said, "No."

POLLACK HOSPITAL

Not much is known about the Pollack Hospital in Bartonville, Illinois. What is known is that it was one of three hospitals on the grounds and it was built in 1949. When you go in for your investigation you get to watch a video about the old hospital and the other connections it has. They make mention of Dr. Zeller who was the first Superintendent at the Peoria State Hospital (many people know it as Bartonville Insane Asylum). However, when you go on the tour at the Pollack Hospital, you find out it was actually the nurse's quarters. They go on to tell you that patients did reside in there at one point when they were over capacity at the hospital.

Before I dive into the Pollack Hospital and our investigation there. I want to make note of our connection with the Peoria State Hospital. When we were coming home from ScareFest in 2013, we came across the Peoria State Hospital. We just happened to get off on an exit to go to a gas station and there it was, right in front of us. Its huge stature and beautiful façade pulled us in. We stopped and took some pictures, felt the energy of the building and got back in the car and headed home.

On the way home, we started to research the building to find out just what this place was. We came across a website that told us it was open for paranormal investigations, however it was $1000 for the night. Yikes, we did not have that type of money to book this location. We figured we would wait a year and then book it.

Fast forward to March 2014, we get a call from another team asking us to team up at the Pollack Hospital in Bartonville, Illinois. To our surprise this was not the structure we had seen in September 2013. We didn't even know the Pollack Hospital existed until this team reached out to us. We didn't care, though, that it wasn't the same building. We were just excited to be investigating an old hospital, and it was connected to the Peoria State Hospital, so who knows what we would come across! Also, in connection with the hospitals are two cemeteries. One is the "old" cemetery, and the other is the "new" cemetery.

The "new" cemetery is massive. There are so many tombstones and it's all in really great condition. We walked around and paid our respects to those who had perished at the hospitals. Someday, I would like to go back and research some of the people within the cemetery. I love to find out more about the people who could potentially be haunting a location we investigate. I love hearing their stories.

The night of the investigation was extremely cold. We were all bundled up in our winter jackets, a few layers of pants, gloves, hats, and scarfs. We started off all together in the basement of the hospital. The basement was just a large room with nothing but concrete surrounding us. We were told there were female spirits down there, so, we tried to get their names. We were not successful.

I think they may have been a little more irritated than excited to talk to us. I was getting the sense from them that they didn't want to speak to *another* group of people. They were tired of people coming in and out of their hospital.

Also, to note, the Pollack Hospital is the "Haunted Infirmary" at Halloween time and is a commercial haunted house. So, there are props and multiple "fake scares" all throughout the hospital. This always makes me wonder if some spirits really get sick of the foot traffic that comes through over time. Maybe this was the "annoyance" I was sensing.

It didn't take long for them to start "kicking" us out. The ghost box kept saying, "Get out." We didn't think anything of this as this is a pretty typical phrase that comes over the ghost box. Then we started hearing knocking on the walls, and the metal door that we were sitting by started to move. It was opening and closing, but only a very small bit. There are no drafts in this basement, either, as there are no windows. Then all of the sudden, we kept hearing things hit the floor, just like something being dropped. We turned on our flashlights to find that buttons were being thrown at us. These were very old buttons, like the ones you would find on an old blazer or suit coat. We thought, "Okay, we better just leave the basement because, clearly, they do not want us down here."

We went upstairs and took a quick break to warm up, and then we split into smaller groups.

Josh, our teammate and I went into a large room on the main floor. This room was setup for the commercial haunt as an "insane asylum". There were a bunch of fake wooden beds, and other hospital attire around. I decided to lay on one of the beds and watch towards the entryway door. We were asking the usual questions, "Who is here with us?" "Can you tell us about yourself?" Not much was happening.

When stuff feels like it's starting to die down we usually just carry on casual conversation. We'll talk about other locations, too, as we found this sometimes sparks activity. It's almost like they don't like you talking about other locations while you're in their domicile.

I was still laying there gazing at the entryway door. It was just a few seconds, and then I saw it. It was this large black mass standing in the doorway. He had unusually long fingers, probably about 9 feet tall (I may be exaggerating on this, but he was taller than anything I had ever seen at this point in time of investigating), and had no facial features. He was quite slender too. He was standing in a "ready-to-go" stance, almost like he was getting ready to attack. His arms were down by his sides, but lifted slightly so you could see between his body and his arms. He was a shadow person, but a very dark and large shadow person. Josh and our other teammate saw him as well.

We all jumped to our feet the minute we saw him. We asked each other, "Are you seeing what I'm seeing?" We jumped up but were stuck in our tracks the minute we got to our feet. This man remained there for about another minute, just gazing upon us. He wouldn't move from the doorway. We were wondering how in the world we were going to get out of this room. We literally couldn't move. I think this may have been out of fear more than he was "holding" us there.

It was just like a breeze came through and whisked him away, because all of the sudden, he just dissipated in the air. This was our time to act and get out of there. We quickly walked to the "safe room" where we were keeping our equipment, and where we could get warm.

We all sat there in silence. I think we were more in shock of what we just saw. When the other team we were investigating with got there we told them about what we saw. They continued to tell us that they saw something of the same description on the other end of the hospital, but it didn't stay and look at them for as long as it looked at us.

We concluded the investigation around 3:00am. We were exhausted and ready to go laydown. We left the hospital, got to our hotel, and we were wide awake. This usually happens. We all discussed the investigation and what we had seen. We wondered if this figure we even saw was human, or was this spirit we came across an elemental.

An elemental spirit was never in the physical world, but they are not a demon. They are more of your "fantasy" type creature or your cryptid type creatures. They are very powerful and do not like to be within a large group of people. You usually find them in quiet areas (which this hospital is definitely in a quiet area). They can put off a very high vibration of energy that can be good or bad. This could have been the energy that kept us stuck in our tracks.

We have yet to return to the Pollack Hospital. I would be interested to see if this slender-like man still resides there, and if he is still a large presence in that building.

KATIE HOPKINS

70

BELVOIR WINERY

Belvoir Winery is definitely in my top five favorite places to investigate. The structure alone is stunning, and the history behind it adds so much character to the building.

The winery was once the Odd Fellows Home in Liberty, Missouri. We were first introduced to the winery when we visited our friends from the CGC; they took us to the winery for some spirits (both wine and paranormal). We had a glass of wine, geared up and went to investigate. Yes, I know people say you shouldn't have alcohol while investigating. This is something we also take seriously, however, one glass of wine was not enough to make us vulnerable. Also, we had our one glass of wine hours before our investigation. We are all smart investigators and we know our limits. Now if we would have sat there and drank glasses upon glasses, we would not have investigated -- one for our safety from the spirits and two, physically.

The main building of the winery is in great shape, and the owners have done an incredible job with renovating it, and creating it into an event center and Inn (in which Josh and I have had the pleasure of staying). As for the other buildings, the nursing home, and hospital, they are deteriorating minute by minute, so we had to be alert and aware of our safety and we needed to know where we were walking. Luckily, we had the best tour guides with Adam and Alec taking us around the buildings.

Also, outside of the buildings to the back, is the Odd Fellows Cemetery. This cemetery pays respects and holds hundreds of the Odd Fellows that lived there for many years.

There is also an Odd Fellow you can see directly in a glass case inside of the main building. His name is George. He was an Odd Fellow and his skeleton is on display in the Winery.

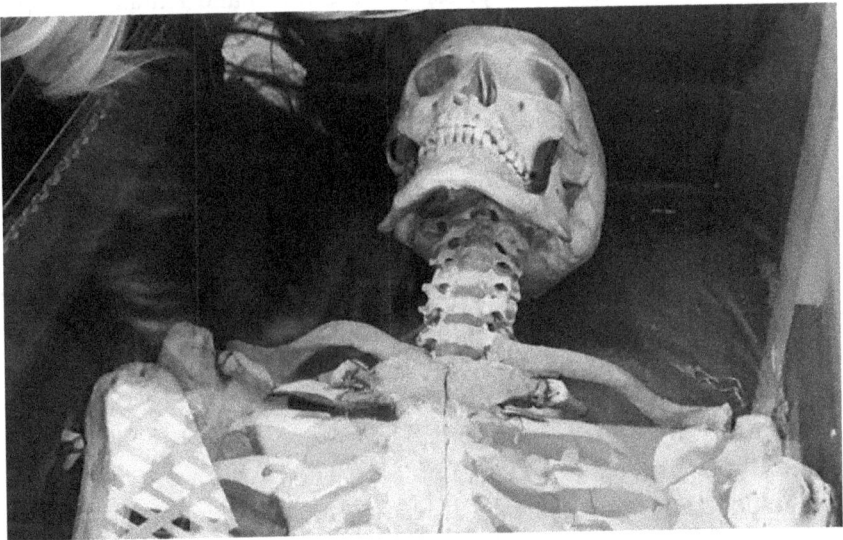

Let's get to the investigating. We started off by walking through all of the buildings, getting a feel for the energy and to get a feel of the structure. The first investigation, honestly, is a blur to me. I'm not sure why. The most recent investigations there within the last two years are much clearer to me.

I remember we went across the "Bridge of Doom" to get into one of the wings of the old hospital. It is called the Bridge of Doom because it is caving in and could collapse at any second. We got across the Bridge of Doom and in that hallway that is across from the bridge there is said to be a portal. A portal is an access or entry way for the paranormal to come into our realm. Please do not associate portal with demonic hauntings only. A portal is merely an entry or access point. The area in that hallway was very heavy and you could definitely feel multiple energies around you. We did not stay long in this area as the energies around us were beginning to become a little much for us, so we carefully crossed the Bridge of Doom and carried on our investigation. This investigation was the first of many at Belvoir and the least of what was to come.

That first investigation was in 2014. In March 2015 we went back to visit our friends and, of course, we made our stop at the Winery. This time it was a group of us which included, Josh, myself, Adam, Alec, Gideon (member of CGC) Hannah (Josh's Sister), Tyler (Hannah's boyfriend at the time) and Hannah Tillery (Adam's wife, girlfriend at the time).

Before we get into the winery investigation, though, I want to discuss some of the occurrences that led up to the investigation. We visit our friends in Kansas not only for investigating but to enjoy time together as friends. The first night Josh and I got to Kansas we went to one of the local bars to watch the Iowa Women's Basketball game. They were in the NCAA tournament, so we had to watch. Adam and Hannah graciously adhered to our desire to watch the game and took us out to this local bar. We sat down, had some drinks and some dinner and the game came on.

Not long after the game was on, the TV right above our table went out. We giggled a little bit because we always seem to have some type of "technical difficulty" when we are with them. Coincidence or paranormal? I'll leave you to decide, but it seems a bit odd that this was the only TV in the bar to go out. Granted, the experiences we would have at Belvoir the next night would be with some electrical fixtures. Thankfully, we were able to watch the game on another TV. I honestly cannot remember if the women won, I think this may have been the Sweet Sixteen game that they lost.

We went on with our evening enjoying the company, went back to our hotel and met up with Adam and Hannah again the next day to head out to Belvoir. Before we headed to Belvoir we decided to go take a tour of the historic Grinter Place.

The Grinter House was built in 1857 and was home to Moses and Annie Grinter. Mr. Grinter operated a ferry boat that went across the Kansas River. He would transport soldiers from Fort Leavenworth and Fort Scott, and many other types of businessmen would use the ferry.

On this tour was Josh, Hannah (sister), and Hannah's boyfriend at the time. The tour is a self-guided tour through the home. We started on the first floor and worked our way up to the second floor. The home already had the "spirit" feeling to it. I'm sure the Kansas River may have something to do with the activity there, since water sources are said to give spirits more energy. Once we got to the second floor of the house, the lights started to flicker. This just added to our list of "technical difficulties" we had over the weekend in Kansas. I am not confirming nor denying that the Grinter House is haunted, but this was a great "electrical" experience to add to our list. I will mention the lights were fine until we got up there. When we would go into a different room, the lights would also stop flickering.

We arrived at Belvoir Winery quite early, so Hannah and I enjoyed a glass of wine and walked the grounds to take it all in. It is so massive and beautiful, even the buildings in their dilapidated state. If you really look at the buildings and soak in their energy, you can "see" them in their original state and how beautiful they were before the elements took their toll on them. We waited for the winery to close to the public and then went into what is called the Ice Cream Parlor. This is where we had our "command central" when we needed a break and stored our equipment that we weren't using.

We started off in the basement of the nursing home, which to my knowledge, had a morgue. The first thing we did was conduct an EVP blast. This is where you record for a short amount of time, about a minute and a half to three minutes and ask questions in a "round robin" style. There was a moment of silence and you can hear me ask in the recording, "If that was you, can you make another knock?"

I want to point out, the area we were in was concrete, and there are no wooden floor boards or anything that could creak. The second I asked for another knock we all heard with our own ears a loud creaking noise. This can be heard on our team's website. There was nothing in that room that could have made that noise, especially not one of us making the noise. We even looked for things to try and recreate the sound and we couldn't find anything that would. This was a great kick off to the start of our investigation.

We decided to take a quick break to warm up since it was fairly cold outside. We got back to the Ice Cream Parlor and we sat down to take a break. All of the sudden, the light above us (there are multiple light fixtures in the Ice Cream Parlor area) was starting to flicker. As soon as this started, Alec turned his camera on. Not only was the light flickering, Alec's fully charged battery started to die. He was able to capture the light flickering and the light completely going out. Once the light went out, his camera shut off.

You can take this how you would like. Was this a sign that there were spirits around using the energy from the light and the camera? With the other happenings at the bar and then now at the winery, we could only think that this had something to do with spirit activity. We cannot fully confirm it, but it was just a very odd experience for the TV to go out, the light to flicker and eventually go out right above us, and along with Alec's fully charged battery dying during all of this.

We, eventually, went back into the cold buildings. We were in the old Odd Fellow's home, which is pictured at the beginning of this section. It has the tree limbs and branches in front of it. We went into one of the hallways that is said to have a woman lingering in the hall. We were conducting another EVP blast and we were able to catch a woman's voice on the recorder. We are still unsure to this day what she is saying, but we can definitely tell that there is a woman's voice. The chill in the air started to take a toll on us so we decided to end the investigation.

We would not return to Belvoir for a few years, and the next time would not be for investigating. It was to celebrate Adam and Hannah's wedding.

MISSOURI STATE PENITENTIARY

I can now say I have been on two private paranormal investigations at the infamous Missouri State Penitentiary (MSP). This was going to be the largest location we had ever investigated, and I am not so sure we were ready. We were ready as investigators, but this place is so massive, that it's overwhelming for even the most veteran investigator. You have to have a plan of action is as far as communication methods go.

My first round at MSP was pretty quiet. We caught a few EVPs and we did have some buttons thrown in the dungeon area, but as far as personal experiences go, we didn't have too many. It was the second visit to MSP that would rock my world of prison investigations. MSP is such an overwhelming location due to its size and the energy that lingers in each building.

I do also want to shout out to the amazing tour guides at MSP. They make your experience so much better with their stories as well, and helping find triggers to bring out the activity. They bring the prison back to life for you during the tours. Our tour guide during the daytime tour was an old prison guard for many years. He now tells his stories of having conversations with the prisoners and is very knowledgeable on the history of the old prison. He tells you many stories of the horrors that went on inside the prison walls, with many inmates being murdered. At the end of the tour, he pulls a bag out from behind the large rails on the wall of the prison. In this bag, he unrolls a red blanket that inside holds multiple shanks. He goes on to tell you that all but two of the shanks you are looking at had killed someone in the prison.

It was when Josh, Sarah, Shannon and I went in May 2015 that we would see and hear what the spirits of MSP have to offer. We are all about the day tours of haunted locations. This is where you get your best stories from people who not only experienced the paranormal activity, but in MSP's case, have experienced the prison when it was alive with inmates. We also toured the museum which is across the street in the old Warden's house. This would be the kickoff to our crazy time at MSP.

Shannon always has a recorder going. Even if it's on a day tour, because you never know what you might catch! We were in the museum, and we were talking to the employee at the museum about the 1954 riot. Long story short, the inmates took over the prison in September 1954 by pretending to be sick, they then beat the guards and stole their keys. This was all in attempt to murder a "snitch" named Walter. They were successful in their attempts. They ran up and down the prison cat walks yelling, "Walter!" and eventually murdered him.

We got back to the hotel after our tour to get ready for the investigation. Shannon came down knocking on our door and was smiling. He said to us, "Listen to this!"

So, we put on the headphones, Shannon pushed play and we heard a voice saying, "Walter!" The "l" and "r" of Walter were drawn out, too.

We quickly got back in the car and drove back to the museum before they closed so we could have the guides listen to what we had caught. Let me bring to your attention, we did not know the name of the inmate that was killed during this riot until we got back to the museum and had them listen to the EVP. The guides gasped for air and were in total shock and excitement when they heard it. They said, "WALTER IS WHO WAS MURDERED IN THE RIOT!"

We all were shocked and excited at what we caught. This EVP can be heard on the Unknown Darkness website as well. This definitely set the tone for the investigation that evening.

We then went back to the hotel again, geared up and headed back about 8:00 PM for the investigation. We started in A Hall, we setup our DVR cameras and then went over to C Hall to investigate. We wouldn't realize what had been going on in A Hall while we were not in there until evidence review. Shannon reviews the DVR evidence and, one day, I got a text message of a photo that said, "Do you see that?"

I sure did see it! It was a photo of a shadow figure on the catwalk in A Hall! We were not in the building at the time we caught it, either, so we could definitely rule out our shadows. The best part is, we even caught the shadow moving!

You can clearly tell as well that the shadow is transparent. Who could this be? Was it one of the old inmates of MPS making his rounds on the catwalk? This is probably the best shadow figure we have caught to date.

Here are some photographs from MSP.

From left to right starting in the back: Shannon, Josh, (Front) Sarah, Katie.

The Colonel Darwin W.
MARMADUKE
HOUSE
(The Warden's Residence)
1888
Listed on
The National Register of Historic Places

KATIE HOPKINS

WORST NIGHTMARES COME TRUE AT BUCHANAN COUNTY HOME

I could probably write an entire book on just my experiences at the Buchanan County Home. I had a hard time remembering all of them, there are so many. So, I will discuss the experiences that have stuck out to me, and clearly there are reasons for that. I am going to separate these stories with subtitles since there are so many of them, and they all lead up to my last experience at the home. This is the section when you will find out why I put "Seeing" Spirits in quotes. I am going to go through this section chronologically as I feel each experience leads up to the next and why my final experience is so terrifying and so memorable.

I will start off with some history about the Buchanan County Home. The Buchanan County Home is the old Poor Farm out near Independence, Iowa. The original building was built in 1861, and housed the incurably insane, disabled, elderly, orphans, the poor, and more. Around 1910, there was a new building built around the old structure, which is the building you will see today. There are still documents, furniture and paintings on the wall in the building to show guests the memories of the patients who lived there.

In the 1880s the Buchanan County Home residents experienced the worst living conditions they could have ever imagined. Vermin, lice, parasites, feces, urine were all present on the residents, and malnutrition was rampant. One resident stated that they saw one of their peers walking down the hallway "covered in vermin." This was under the supervision of the Samson's. They were eventually cut as the Stewards of the home, but eight years later were re-elected.

In the 1970s the home was shut down and the residents were moved to the nearby hospital or mental health institute. The Buchanan County Sheriff's Office took over the second and third floor of the building as their offices and training headquarters. There was a holding cell as well in the building. They occupied the building up until the late 2000s.

In the most recent years, the building was occupied by a monk, but we wonder about his "status" as a monk. He ended up fleeing in the middle of the night and left behind documents and belongings. He was wanted for not paying multiple bills, among other things. The most outrageous thing we found from the monk's time were documents of women being in the monastery. It seemed to be more of a "cult" than anything.

Uncovering the Past

Josh and I decided to go research the Buchanan County Home one day at the Buchanan County Genealogical Society. We were going through microfilms, old newspapers, ledgers, and even obituaries from the home. We came across some very disturbing history while researching. This is when we came across the Samson's time as the stewards of the home. We read about all of the horrors that went on as they were in charge. It made my skin crawl reading about the conditions of the home and what it had to be like for the patients there. We had read and heard of mistreatment of patients during this time in other facilities, but we didn't expect to find it in one of the facilities to which we had access.

We decided after we were done researching that we might as well head to the building to do some investigating. This was a 45-minute drive for us, so being so close we had to go to the building.

The First Experience

The first experience I would have at the Buchanan County Home makes me wonder now if this spirit we encountered would be the one to change the paranormal field for me forever. Josh and I went out to the home in the early fall of 2013. Not many investigations had been done at the home, so we were curious to see what we would find and or experience. We started in the "basement" area, which is really just a shelter area, and a laundry room; it's quite small. We stood at the bottom of the stairs and started to conduct a ghost box session. Josh said something about one of the Samson's coming over the ghost box and over the ghost box we got, "Evil."

Josh looked shocked, and I laughed. I am not sure why I laughed, but apparently, I thought it was funny that they were reacting to him saying, "It's probably Samson coming over the ghost box."

Could this be they were saying they were evil people, or was this something evil letting us know they were coming for us? The next session of our investigation would sum that up for us.

Josh and I eventually made our way to the second floor where the chapel is. The chapel has always had a weird feeling to it. You can sense the energy in the walls every time you walk in there, and you can only wonder what happened in here. There is a small crawl space on the left side of the alter that has a hidden door and leads into another room. The room cannot be any bigger than 10x10, but the ceiling is high. We believe this was installed when the monk took over the building, and we still to this day wonder for what that room was used.

We were standing at the back of the chapel and we were just feeling out the space. We only had a recorder and camera going at this time. The room kept getting darker and darker, and we began to hear footsteps and other noises, which were not the building shifting. The darkness was almost too much to handle, so at that time we decided to call one of our other teammates. We wanted to see if they could remote view what we were feeling, however, they didn't answer so we just kept on with our investigation.

About 20 minutes later, the room got so heavy it was almost unbearable. I was about ready to tell Josh that I thought we needed to leave, when all of the sudden right behind him was a huge black mass standing there. This made me jump so high you thought I could jump high enough to play NBA basketball.

Josh immediately asked, "What?"

I told him what I saw. This black mass was lingering behind him, it had to of been about 8 feet tall and extremely wide. I had never seen anything like it in my few years of investigating at that time. That was the icing on the cake; we had to get out of there.

We ran so fast down the stairs to the cafeteria area, grabbed our stuff and left. We didn't even look back.

Once we got off of the property, barely off the driveway, our other teammate called me and asked what was going on. I told him about the experience in the chapel, and he said that what he saw was the building in shambles. Crumbled and reeking of waste. What did this mean? We had no idea. He thought maybe it was the energy from the patients who were there during the 1880s.

In my mind, I was thinking it was whatever we just saw in the chapel. It was pure evil. I want to explain to, you can experience evil and it not be demonic. What we were dealing with I do not believe was demonic. I think things would have been a lot worse, but I think we were dealing with someone or something that had evil written all over them. Just like a bad person can be evil in their human state, this spirit was still evil in their afterlife. I do not know to this day if we were dealing with an elemental spirit or if it was someone who had passed on and just emitted that much negative energy.

The next night, Josh and I decided to go back. I know, we're crazy. But we were so curious as to what happened the night before we had to get some more answers. I was scared out of my mind going back, but I was too curious and I wanted to know what that black mass had been.

Josh and I pulled into the drive of the home, the place where we parked our car was to the side of the building, near the back entrance. We sat there, stared at the building, talked about how we were going to approach the situation, carried on more conversation, looked at the building again... we couldn't get out of the car. The energy, even just looking at the building, was so powerful that it kept us from getting out.

Let me remind you, this was a 45-minute drive one way for us, so an hour and a half total. We tried so hard to reach for the car door handles, but we couldn't. I just sat there staring at the building, and the evil we had experienced the night before was pounding on the car keeping the doors shut. I look back at this now and wonder, was it the evil keeping us in the car, or was there a spirit looking out for us keeping us in the car because they knew of the evil that lurked inside?

I will never know, but I'm thankful we didn't go in. There's always a reason for something. That something that night was us not going into that evil-infested building.

CEMETERY SEARCHING

Josh and I knew about the Poor Farm Cemetery that was right off of the main road leading to the home. You can see it right from the street. Our curiosity lied within the Poor Farm Cemetery that you cannot see or get to from the road. You have to hike, or drive through a corn field in my tiny little Chevy Malibu. I'm pretty sure our curiosity lead to my Malibu not working so great in its later years. This cemetery dates back to the beginning of the poor farm. There is a sign right off of the road that gives you information about it, but you cannot see the cemetery. We were told by Josh's uncle that we had access to it since it was property of the home, so we decided to go on a little hike.

POOR FARM CEMETERY
THE BUCHANAN COUNTY "POOR FARM"
WAS ESTABLISHED IN 1861, AND RECEIVED ITS
FIRST RESIDENTS IN 1867.
THE FIRST DEATH OF A RESIDENT OCCURRED
IN 1868, AND A CEMETERY WAS ESTABLISHED
BEHIND THIS FIELD.
THIS CEMETERY REMAINED IN USE UNTIL 1942.
ABOUT 35 PEOPLE ARE BURIED HERE,
AMONG THEM ONE CIVIL WAR VETERAN.

ACCESS
RESTRICTED

We started off by going through a pasture, which was full of cows, this may have been the scariest part of searching for the cemetery. I didn't want to get trampled by a disgruntled cow. We eventually made our way deep into the forest, I really felt like I was on an episode of *Lost* or something, or a reality show about venturing into the woods to find only God knows what. We stumbled across an old nearly-empty creek. We went looking through it seeing if we could find any old artifacts, and we did!
We found an old shoe that looks to be dated back to maybe the 1930s to 1940s era and an old sign that says, "Buchanan Co. Care Facility Independence, IA."

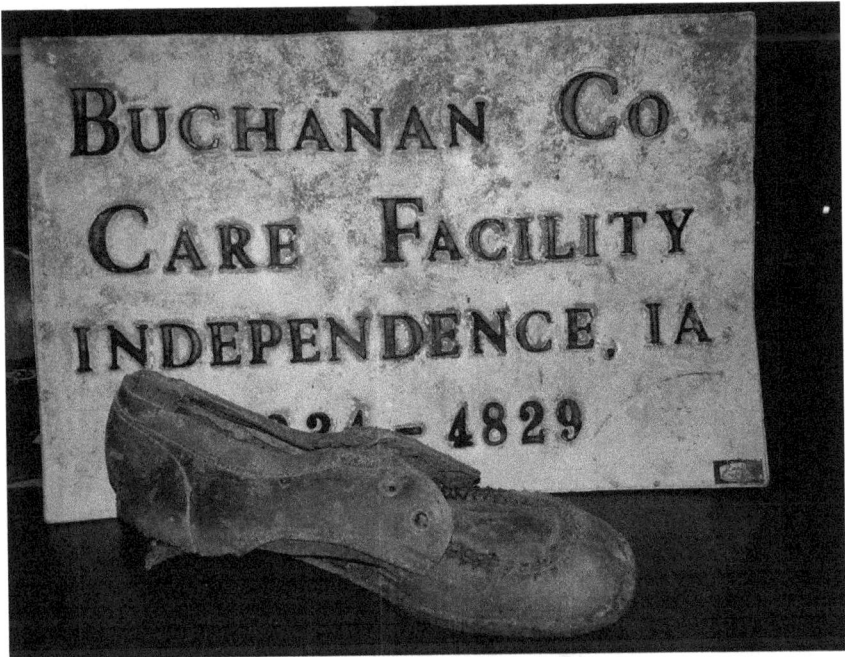

We were so excited to find such artifacts. We also wondered, was this a sign that we have a connection to that building that is so strong it allowed us to find these items?
The shoe to this day gets me. How was this shoe in the middle of a creek for this long and we are the ones that just so happen to find it?

Not only did we find these items, we also found bones and deer antlers. I think the bones we found were animal bones, but it does add to the adrenaline when you're cemetery-searching. We packed up the items in a bag we had with us and carried on to find the cemetery.

We were walking for probably about an hour, and we could not find the cemetery. Did we go too far? Did we not go far enough? We had no clue. We thought we had an idea of where it was from the sign on the street, but we are no Lewis and Clark.

We started to get a little scared that we weren't even going to find our way out. Then, we came across a small grassy area that almost looked like an aisle, and it lead to the back of a fence. We walked up to it and there it was, the Old Poor Farm Cemetery!

We were so excited, we got into the cemetery and we started looking at all of the tombstones. There are actually maps that show the plots of the tombstones, only by numbers though, no names. On the plot map it shows about 40 people buried in the cemetery, but there are only about 7 tombstones left. The numbered tombstones are just made out of old concrete, with the number etched into it.

However, there was one tombstone that stuck out to us. It was perfectly white, and it had a name on it. "St. Clair Edward: 1843, May 29 1915: Veteran Confederate States of America".

This caught Josh and I way off guard. Not only about it being a soldier buried in a poor farm cemetery, but it was a soldier from the Confederate States of America. We still do not know much about Edward St. Clair, other than that he was born in Louisiana which explains him fighting for the Confederacy, but we do not know why he came to Buchanan County, Iowa, after the war.

98

In my thoughts, I'm wondering if he was a POW of the Civil War and was in the North and when he was released, he decided to stay here? We may never know and that will take a lot more research. Hopefully someday Josh and I can find the story on him. As a history buff, this was such an incredible find, for both Josh and I. We share a love for the paranormal, but also for history. No wonder we are such a great match!

We probably could have spent hours upon hours in that cemetery. We know that there are some unmarked graves there as well, since there were so few tombstones, and in the plot map it shows around 40 being buried there. We paid our respects, snapped some more pictures, and nightfall was coming so we decided we better start our hike back since we didn't know the woods very well.

We were still hiking, and it was getting dark. This added to the scare factor of being in the woods in the dark, surrounded by cows, and who knows what else. We may have put ourselves in more danger that day and night than we realized.

We went back to the home, and we reflected on everything we encountered that day. We were observing the sign we found and the shoe. The soul of the shoe was nailed to the actual leather part of the shoe. This we found odd, and only added to the curiosity we had about it. Was this shoe thrown out or did this shoe rise from the ground from one of the patients from the Buchanan? Who knows how long it had been there, and we were the ones who just so happened to find it!

We did not investigate that night since we were extremely tired from the hike and all of the emotions that went through us that day, whether we realized it or not. I think our findings that day though would continue into some experiences we would have to come at the home.

THE DARKNESS RETURNS

In November 2013 we held a public event at the home, so a few weeks before the event, we wanted to go out and try to scrounge up some more evidence with which wow our guests. It was Josh, our two teammates at the time and myself.

We started off the night in the basement area of the home. It was myself and the other female investigator that was on our team at the time, standing next to each other in the laundry room. Josh and the other male investigator were standing right in front of us. The night started off active with bangs, miscellaneous noises and voices. It took no longer than five minutes in that laundry room to set the mood for the night.

While we were standing there, all of the sudden my teammate and I jumped back at the same time. We both looked at each other and both asked, "What did you just see?"

What we saw I think would scar us for a while, if not still to this day. As we were standing there conducting an EVP session, we both saw a large figure crawl in between us, which made us both jump back at the same time. When she asked what I saw, I said, "It was crawling!"

She then started laughing and yelled, "Yes!"

It looked as though it was an adult on all fours crawling at us at a really fast pace. Josh also saw this figure, but it wasn't as close to him as it got to the other investigator and I. This would not be the only run-in with this crawling figure either. It was probably about five feet tall, its back was curled and its spine was sticking out (just as if someone was so skinny you can see every notch of their spine). There really were no facial features to it, just a blank dark black face. If I could put a face on it though, I would say droopy eyes, crooked smile, I definitely know it was smiling, the way it made us jump! It also had long fingers and long toes. It was very mutant-like.

This also would not be the craziest activity we witnessed that night. We decided to go up to the attic. The attic is filled with old pieces of furniture from when it was the poor farm.

It also includes what looks to be as some type of bird cage. We all have our theories on this cage though. A lot of activity would also be focused around that cage for the rest of the evening and within the beams in the ceiling in the attic.

When we got up to the attic we could feel the energy was a lot different than it was down in the laundry area. The laundry area was not as heavy, and the attic felt like we were all being weighed down with 1000 pounds of bricks. The other female investigator that was with us would be the one to feel it the worst that night. We all kept seeing a figure jumping from beam to beam and messing with us. It would even go into the cage and rattle it. It had a very dark, ominous presence to it, but we kept moving forward to see if we could figure what or who we were dealing with.

The K2 meter started to go off, but there is no electricity up in the attic. There are two extremely terrifying parts to this portion of this investigation. The first one would be with the other female investigator being taken over by this dark entity, the other would be in evidence review when we heard what was going on that we could not hear at that point in time during the investigation.

I'll begin with the first part, and our teammate being taken over. She was always open to the dark part of the paranormal. She loved researching dark hauntings and was open to them, almost too open in this case. The attic kept getting heavier and heavier; I'm not sure how it was even possible. All of the sudden, I looked over to my teammate and saw her staring to the back of the attic. I tried to get her attention, saying her name a few times. She would not answer me, so I grabbed her arm and shook her a little bit and said her name again. She looked at me and said, "Hmm."

She had an evil look on her face, almost to where her face was not hers, and she smiled at me. I told Josh and our other teammate that we had to get out of there and we had to, most importantly, get *her* out of there. She almost walked robotically, and she would not take her eyes off of the back of the attic.

We got her down the stairs to the cafeteria area, and she still would not get out of this trance like state. So, we got her in the car, put crystals in her hand, and drove to the nearest church. We said Saint Michael's prayer and then all of the sudden, she looks at me and asked, "Why are we in a church parking lot?"

I told her what had just happened and she didn't believe me. She said we were just investigating in the attic and things were fine. I told her, no they were not fine, and she had just been taken over by whatever was up there. She would not believe us until we showed her the video. I think she was more in shock of what had happened than we.

We went back to the home since we left our equipment there, left her in the car while we packed up, and we left. We did not want to see what else could possibly happen that night.

When we got home and went through our video and audio recorders. We heard a deep voice say her name. This voice was so dark and terrifying. There was also a voice that came across that said, "And wanting me."

We still do not know to what this was in reference. Maybe it was referring to our teammate wanting to witness this dark entity and what it could do?

Our teammate was affected by that for quite some time. We didn't go back to the home until our event which was in later November, and we did not let her go up to the attic. It is probably the only time I've ever told someone in this field to close their mind. I did not mean to close her mind off to the paranormal, but to the dark entity that wanted to take her over so badly, to not let it get to her. This was for the safety of not only her, but for our guests.

WRECKAGE AWAKENS

This section of the stories about the Buchanan County Home is not necessarily paranormal-focused. This section is to inform those of the vandalism that occurred at the home. It also leads up to my final story about "seeing" spirits. In August 2014, the home was broken into by local high school kids. They vandalized the building so badly, that some portions of the building were beyond repair.

Pictured below is broken glass from the third-floor stair doors.

The vandals also spray-painted satanic symbols which included a pentagram, the numbers "666" and even wrote "die" on the wall with spray paint. They also attempted to write the word "Satan" in the chapel but their spelling failed them and they wrote "Satin". They even lit a mattress on fire in the outside brick shed building. Luckily this structure was brick, otherwise there could have been a lot more damage. The mattress that was lit on fire was the one from the attic that you saw in a previous photo.

You may ask why I am including this in a book about my paranormal experiences. Well one, I want people to understand and see the damage. Pictures do not even remotely show the amount of damage that was done. Two, I believe that the vandalism has something to do with the amount of activity we had after this was done.

We went out to the Buchanan in August 2014, with the hopes to investigate the building, and to try and collect the answers we longed for about all of the previous activity we had. Instead, we spent the night talking with officers and assessing the damage that had been done.

Finally, I added this into this book to bring awareness about security for historic buildings. These vandals not only caused physical damage, but this hurt us emotionally. I have seen so many locations with vandalism damage done to them over the years. I hope those who read this will help bring awareness to show the importance of security for these buildings. Also, the historical value these buildings have. How could anyone do this to such a beautiful structure? If your plan is to just destroy history, stay away! Luckily, the vandals were found and were arrested. They are facing felony charges.

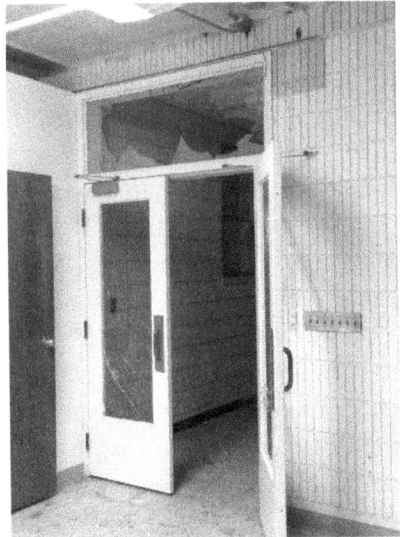

"Seeing" Spirit

Finally, you will now hear the story that makes me put "seeing" into quotes. This story has been featured in the book *Encounters With The Paranormal: Volume 3*. I am going to rearrange this story a little bit and talk about the events leading up to my most terrifying experience, to date, in the paranormal field.

I believe that all of this started from our first experience back in the fall of 2013, when Josh and I witnessed the black mass in the chapel. Then there was the experience with our teammate being taken over, followed but the vandalism adding the negative energy that was put into the walls that night. The man I was about to encounter in July 2015, I think had everything to do with all of those events. He just wasn't ready for me to "see" him until now.

Let me define "see" in quotes. If you have researched the paranormal field and know about the "third eye," this is what I am talking about. The third eye allows you to visualize and see spirit in your mind. I cannot open up my eyes and see them physical standing in front of me, but I can picture them in my mind and see their details, personality and even feel their emotions. I do not consider myself a medium or a psychic, but sensitive and an empath. We all have empathic abilities, we just have to learn how to use them, and apparently, the paranormal field has taught me just that. I had always been sensitive to spirits when I first started off in the field, I could feel their presence, but I could not visualize them as clear as I can now. I think the more open you become and the more you're willing to accept that you have these abilities, the more powerful they get. When I say powerful, I mean making it easier to visualize them and "see" them.

I always get a little shaky and nervous writing about this experience, as I do not want to open up anymore to this guy as I have already. If I never encounter him again, I would be okay with that. I still have yet to figure out if he is stuck at the Buchanan or if he would be able to make his way to another location where he would be "welcomed." I would not welcome him, but if there are other dark spirits willing to bring him in, could he go there?

In July 2015, Josh, Hannah (sister), Tyler (ex-boyfriend), Joy (Mom), and a few neighbor friends went out to investigate. The night started off pretty quiet, nothing really happening, not even feelings of being watched. We decided to go walk around and get more of a feel for the building to see if we could find the "hotspots" that night. We didn't like to go in certain areas, as the holes in the glass on the doors now allowed for the bats that were in the attic to come down to the main floors. So we decided to go to the stairs that were on the second floor, just down from the chapel. There was a landing at the top of them that then turned to another set of stairs leading to the third floor. The door to the third floor that was at the top of the stairs is in the vandalism pictures.

We started to conduct an EVP blast to see if we could even get any voices coming across that. There was not much; we almost were ready to call it quits. Tyler and I were sitting on the second floor stairs, about three stairs up. Then I felt it, the dark, ominous, vile, disgusting feeling this guy puts off. I could "see" him coming down the stairs from the third floor. He was slowly making his way down, and then he got to the landing of the stairs. He started to peek around the wall, just looking Tyler and I over, sizing us up, wondering what move we'll make next and what he could do to us.

He smiled this crooked, gnarly grin, and that's when I said, "Tyler get up now!"

Tyler and I stood up as fast as we could, and I told everyone what I had seen. I didn't know what to think at the time since this was the most vivid vision I had ever had. I had never "seen" a spirit that close and that detailed before. I also had never felt more terrified from a spirit like I had from him.

We got up and Tyler started to complain about his back hurting and that it was really hot. So we looked at Tyler's back and found scratch marks in the shape of a backwards "L". There were two marks going down and three marks across. This was a large, raised scratch, too. There is no possible way Tyler could have done this to himself. If you think you can recreate this scratch, be my guest.

This was the last straw. I was done with this guy. I told everyone we needed to leave before something worse happened. My question, though, is why Tyler? If I was the one seeing him, and feeling him, why didn't he do this to me? Instead, he decided to pick on Tyler who couldn't see him or feel him. I was keeping these feelings to myself, too, since I could "see" him coming down the stairs. I didn't want to sound crazy, not have people believe me, and/or scare anyone. Now I know, I should have been telling them all along what I was "seeing."

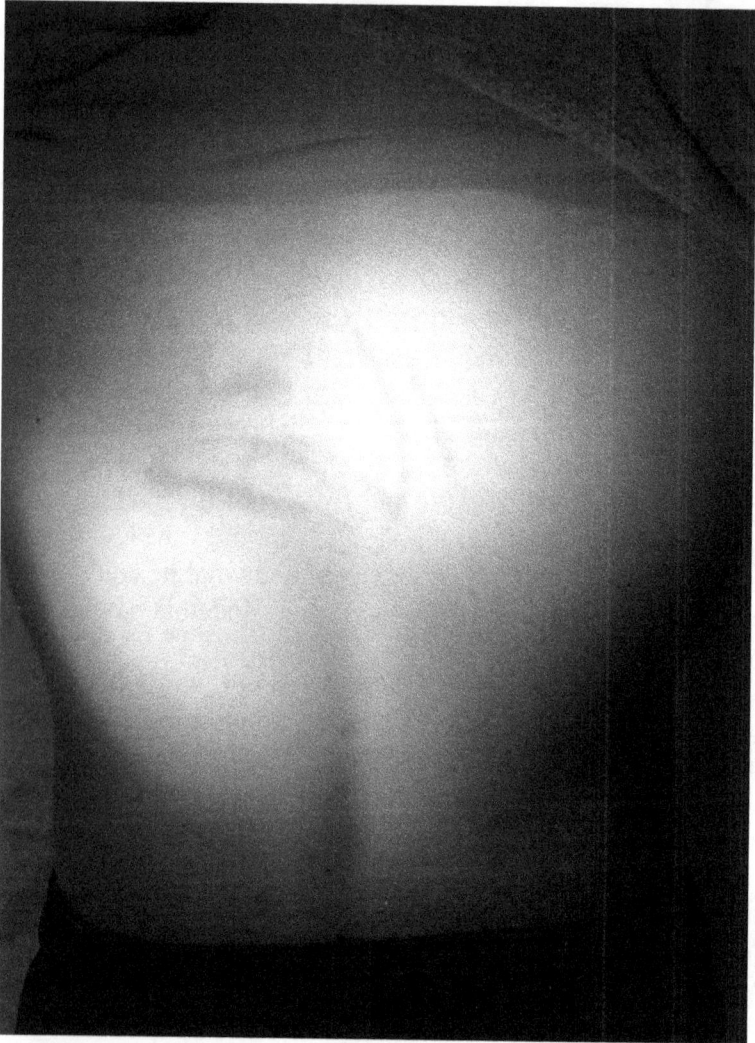

This was the last time I was at the Buchanan County Home, and I never intend to go back. The way this man made me feel was nothing like I had felt before. I didn't want to feel his anger, hatred, and malice again. This is the most terrifying experience I have ever had in the paranormal field. Even with it being the most terrifying, I also thank the spirit for giving me this experience since I have now been able to practice more with my third eye. I have been able to help spirits and I have been able to help my fellow investigators stay safe. I'm so thankful that I have opened up and accepted that I can "see" spirit. In addition, I am also thankful for those who inspired me to write this book, so others can feel comfortable opening up about their abilities.

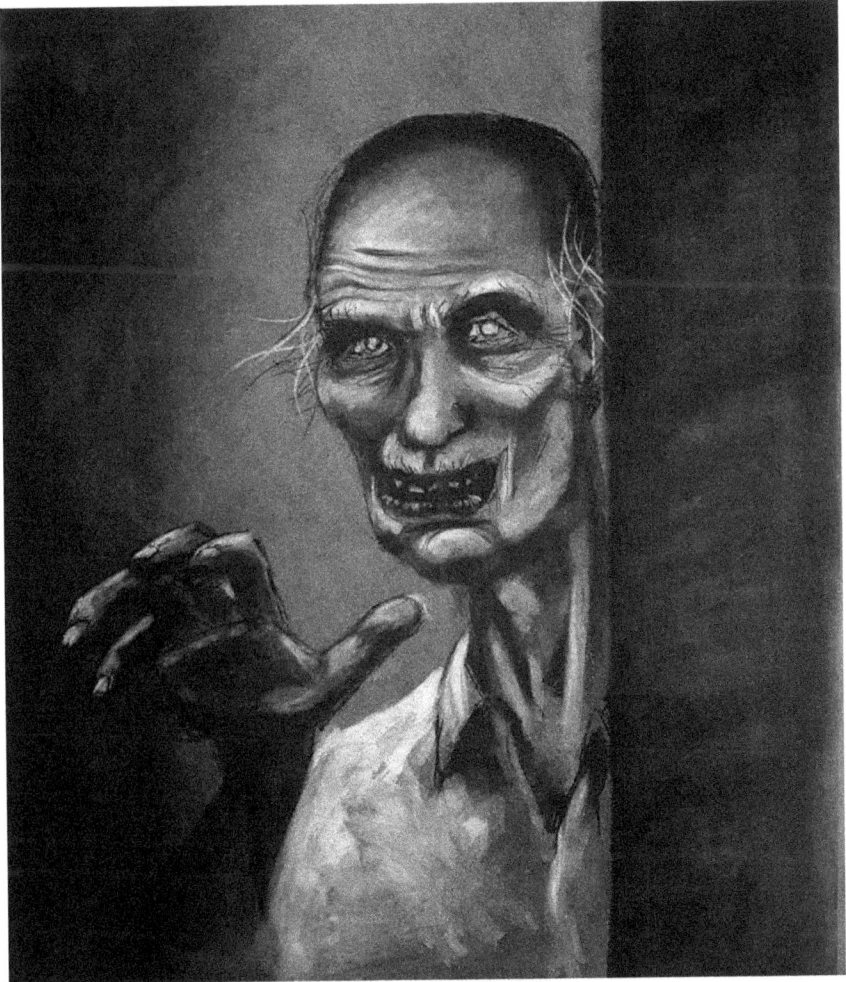

"SEEING" OTHER SPIRITS

This next section is going to be a compilation of many experiences I have had in the paranormal field. I will break these up by the name of the location. Some locations have asked to remain undisclosed, so I will title those with an experience there.

BREMER COUNTY POOR FARM

The Bremer County Poor Farm (known as the Poor Farm Foundation Building today), was built in 1953, however the land on where the current building sits dates back to 1890 with the old Poor Farm. The history there is very dark which includes a mother murdering her own children in cold blood. Also, the maintenance man passed away in the boiler/coal room. This would be the area that we got the most activity.

It was in July 2014, that we were called upon to go investigate the Poor Farm with another team who had been lucky enough to get in contact with the owners. The Poor Farm today runs as the Poor Farm Foundation, but also it has apartments inside, as well. When we investigated there was only one family living in the home and they shared with us the experiences they had been having.

The daughter had experienced seeing shadow people, her door slamming to her bedroom, and the usual feelings of being watched. The parents mentioned how they would hear voices every so often and even would see shadow figures in the hallways. They would have to go to another room in the building to do laundry, and they hated walking to the room by themselves. They would usually go on a "buddy system" to the laundry room for safety.

We got to the poor farm early so we could take a day tour. The poor farm is off of the old highway 218 and there are many evergreen trees surrounding it. We were welcomed by a very unhappy chicken. This got us moving quickly to get inside. The last thing we wanted was to be attacked by a chicken. If I could put a hashtag in here it would say, "Only in Iowa."

We got inside the building and right away we could feel the energy bursting off of the walls. There was happiness, sadness, anger, greed, and hatred, just to name a few of the feelings we had when we walked in there.

We started off on the main floor where there is a corridor that has history related documents (which talks about the mother who killed her children), and other articles that talk about the history of the building and the residents that lived there. Not all are unhappy and terrible stories. There are actually a lot of happy and fun stories to read about. They took great care of their residents at the poor farm. You can definitely feel their energy in the building as well.

The first room we went to on the tour was the boiler/coal room. This room was one of the areas in which we would have the most activity. One of the maintenance men died in this room. He had a heart attack and collapsed. There is a lot of feeling of remorse in the boiler/coal room. Maybe this is because he died tragically? We were hoping to find out why it felt like this during our investigation.

We started our investigation on the second floor. The second floor has individual rooms, but then also two large community rooms. We began in the hallway right outside of the community room on the east side of the building. We started off with conducting an EVP session and we also had the K2 in the doorway of the community room. There was not much happening, at least with personal experiences. However, when we listened back to the audio recorder, we caught a woman's voice. Unfortunately, what she was saying was too difficult to make out.

We continued asking questions and then all of the sudden, the K2 meter started to go off. It would go from green to yellow, then from green to red. We asked if this person was a resident of the poor farm, and it did not go off. We asked if he or she was from "outside" and had made their way to the poor farm, and it went up to red.

There are many times on investigations you will come across spirits who have nothing to do with the location. There are many earthbound spirits that can make their way from location to location. We never did find out from where this spirit had come, but we did find out that it was a woman and she dated back to around 1920. This would have been before the current poor farm building was there. It's extremely important to remember on investigations to not limit the spirits to just the building in which you are. What I mean by this is you may have spirits there that were on the land before the building you are in was even there. If you limit yourself to only location history and not land or area history, you may miss out on communicating with some spirits. Do not have a "fixed' mindset when it comes to locations.

One location that comes to mind that people focus on only specific spirits is the Villisca Axe Murder House. To be quite honest, I do not think the Moore Family, Stillinger's or the murderer are still in that home. We'll get to that story later.

My point is, keep an open mind. You may run into spirits that had nothing to do with the location or land. They may have come from somewhere completely different, but find comfort or sanctuary at that specific location!

Once the spirit up on the second floor had had enough communication with us, we made our way to the first floor. There are again, multiple individual rooms, and a community/library room. The first floor was pretty quiet, so we decided to make our way to the boiler/coal room.

We had the ghost box going. The room still had the feeling of remorse, so we went with that. We asked what happened in there, and we heard over the ghost box, "Died."

This got our adrenaline pumping, so we kept going with it. We were respectful in our questions and wanted to make sure we didn't upset the spirit to whom we were speaking. We never did get the name of the spirit, but many of the things he was saying led us to believe it was the maintenance man. It is believed that the most common "way" to become a spirit is to die tragically, or to have unfinished business. It makes sense that the maintenance man would still be there since he died so tragically and in the spot in which we were standing.

It was starting to get really late, and we were all exhausted from our energy being used to help the spirits communicate with us that night. We also had an hour and a half drive ahead of us, so we decided to call it a night. We paid our respects to the spirits in the home and packed up. We reflected on the activity that we had experienced on our way home. That usually helps us be alert on our drive home after an investigation. We would eventually look into going back to the Bremer County Poor Farm, however, it had been taken over by new owners and it was very difficult to get a hold of them. We still hope to return someday, when the time is right.

HARRIS HAVEN HAUNTED HOUSE

In April 2015, our current team was asked to investigate the Harris Haven Haunted House. Yes, this is a commercial haunted house that people pay to go to for a good scare during Halloween. However, the owner expressed to us that it was not just fake haunts that were in this building. Of course, we wanted to check it out. The element of fear would definitely be at a high since we would turn the corner and see a zombie or some sort of ghoulish figure.

The evening started off quiet, as they usually do. Spirits are just like people, they have to warm up to you to start talking. Keep in mind, spirits were once in our living realm. It's important to approach them just like you would a living human being with respect.

There is a part of the haunted house that is a corn field, with an old house façade at the end of it, where you stand on what looks like a deck. Sarah, a fellow investigator of ours on the Unknown Darkness team, and I were standing on the deck. We kept seeing a dark figure up in the rafters of the building. It would move from the left to the right, then closer to us. It had glowing eyes; you couldn't miss it.

All of the sudden we felt a huge bang come from underneath us. We, again, were standing on the deck portion of this house that's in the corn field area. The area underneath us was nothing but dirt and we were no more than maybe three feet off the ground. Nothing could have gotten under there to make that loud of a bang.

It made us move quickly and then investigate to see what it was. The energy in the room got a little bit darker, and we kept investigating. We got some pretty frightening EVPs of some dark growly voices, and we caught the bang on the recorder and on video.

After this incident we decided to split up, Shannon (Sarah's husband and also another teammate of ours), Josh and a few others that were tagging along with us decided to go in while we took a break. They went up the stairs that are right at the beginning of the haunt, and at the top of the stairs is a hand-drawn picture, by the owner's brother, of a demon. If this didn't make you want to run out the doors, the things they caught on the Ovilus 5 will. They got "sacris" which also means "sacred" in Latin. They got "devil," "evil," "hell," "server," and many other dark words across the Ovilus 5.

Let me go back to when the experiences started for the owner of the haunt. He and a friend were working on the house during the off season, and they started discussing *Revelations* in the Bible, which discusses disaster and suffering. They also discussed fallen angels fornicating with the living. I do not know how they got on this subject, and I never cared to know how or why they got on this subject. However, this is when the owner started to witness activity.

The first experience he had was seeing a large black figure floating in the rafters of the building. He said it stared at him and then disappeared. We did not know of this story until we arrived for our first investigation. This does kind of put everything into perspective. Was their conversation a way to create a "portal" for paranormal activity? Also, the setting in which this conversation took place is a place to cause fear -- usually dark, negative entities thrive on fear. This place is like a magnet for them!

We held a few more investigations at the haunt, and each were darker and darker. We even held an event there in which our guests experienced seeing shadow people and they caught some great EVPs. The owner did eventually take down the drawing of the demon, since this could have been the cause for the negative energies in the building. We have not been back to the haunt since July 2016.

THE ELLIS HOUSE

In the fall of 2016, a co-worker of mine at the time found out that I was a paranormal investigator. So he shared his experiences with me about a house he used to work at. It was then called the Lion and Lamb Bed and Breakfast in Vinton, Iowa. He would create events there and even lived in the basement there with his family for a while. He was able to get us in for an investigation of the house.

The home was built in 1892 by W.C. Ellis. It served as a home and even an apartment complex, until it was created into a nursing home. After the nursing home is when it became the Lion and Lamb Bed and Breakfast. It is once again a private residence.

We completed our first investigation in the early fall of 2016. We were able to witness some personal experiences and catch a few EVPs, nothing that was too crazy or overbearing. It wasn't until we held our event that I would have a vision of some spirits in the home.

We were in one of the rooms that belonged to W.C. Ellis' son. In this room were a few of our event guests and Josh and I. I was sitting on the bed, Josh was standing next to me and the event guests were near the wall that is next to the door. In the corner to the left when one walks in the door there is an old chair. All of a sudden, I started to have a vision of an elderly woman sitting in that chair. She had white hair and a lot of wrinkles on her face. The stress over the years had taken a toll on her. She also had piercing blue eyes. She didn't seem sad, though. She seemed relaxed. She had a lot of excess skin hanging from her arms, giving the indication that at one time was a little heavier. She was dressed in what looked like a nighty pajama outfit. It had a floral pattern on it with pastel pink and blue.

I again, kept this vision to myself, and then one of the event guests said, "I feel like there is something in the corner just staring at me."

I then proceed to tell them all what I saw. They were all in shock when I told them this. They didn't know of my abilities to "see" spirits, so they asked a lot of questions. They were all very supportive, though.

Our time at the Ellis House came to an end after this investigation since the house was up for sale and a family purchased the home. I do wonder if they ever experience any activity today. For some reason, I feel they do, and that it is probably the Ellis' wondering who is in their home and happy to see it thriving again!

German Encounters

Our team has been very fortunate to investigate some of the most amazing historical locations in the Midwest. Shannon is a whiz when it comes to sniffing out locations. That is why you will find we have quite a few "undisclosed" locations. The owners have trusted us enough to come in and investigate, but do not want to be bombarded with calls and emails from other teams. It is definitely an honor and privilege to be able to have access to such amazing places.

One of these locations is located in Western Illinois. It was once a place for Civil War Soldiers to take rest and, also, for sailors to come and have some R&R. It was also, at one time, a school for German children. They would come and learn English and basic reading, writing and arithmetic. We used this information to our advantage while investigating, trying to trigger activity.

We started off on the main floor right above where our "command central" was for the night. We completed a few EVP blasts but didn't get much. We then decided to split up, the guys stayed on the main floor and Sarah and I went up a floor. We were freezing since it was in the middle of December and there was no heat in this building, so we decided to go down to the command central area and sit by the fire.

Josh and Shannon continued on with their investigation. They had the Ovilus 5 going and the word "synn" came across it. They didn't understand what that meant, so they quickly got their phones out and searched for it on the Internet. It means "sin" in German.

They were both thrown back as the dictionary in the Ovilus 5 should only be English words. So this brought to our minds that maybe some children or teachers there are from when it was a German School. But why would it say, "Sin?"

Was it trying to tell us something that went on in the school? We still do not know to this day, but we are heading back to the location again soon! Hopefully, it won't be so cold so we can stay and get some more answers.

Sarah and I warmed up, threw on some more layers and decided to go up by the old bell tower, also known as a cupola in the Victorian Era, basically a watch tower. There are still stairs that lead up to it, but they are very curvy and rickety. Shannon and Josh were brave enough to climb up, but we weren't. Anyway, it was just us two up there and the atmosphere started to get a little bit heavier. It was not a negative heavy, but just a sense of there was someone else with us that we couldn't see... yet. Sarah and I were both trying to communicate with whoever was there with us, asking questions, and carrying on casual conversation. This is when we both saw a figure on the stairs near the top of the cupola. We both jumped back as he came out of nowhere, and Shannon and Josh were watching us on the DVR cameras and could tell that we had just witnessed something.

I was able to get a good "look" at him, and I describe him as about 6 feet tall, husky build, jet black hair, stressed or confused face, and in a low-ranking Union Soldier Uniform. He looked disheveled, as if he had just gotten out of battle. He quickly disappeared, and Sarah and I were freezing cold again, but our adrenaline was at its highest. We decided to go back down to talk to Shannon and Josh to tell them about the experience we'd just had.

It was not an experience that made us feel scared or worried for our safety, but it was more of a surreal experience and that we had just seen a full apparition above us. We hope that with a return visit we can figure out who this gentleman had been and hear his story.

"SEEING" At FULL StRENGtH ONCE AGAIN

We have had the pleasure of meeting so many great people in this field, and the person that reached out to us about this undisclosed location actually messaged us and asked us to investigate. This location has such a rich history, once a county jail, and now a museum. The county jail dates back to the 1890s and there are ledgers in the museum that you can read that tell you who the inmates were and what their crimes had been.

The first vision I had a vision when we got there was of a man hanging in one of the jail cells. I immediately asked the tour guide (who is also a friend of ours from the field) if someone committed suicide in that cell, and I pointed to the cell in which I was "seeing" him. She said, "Yes."

I asked her if he had hung himself, and she said, "Yes."

I then asked her about the decade in which he'd committed the act, if it had been the 1970s and she, also, said, "Yes."

I began to ask her a few more questions while I was also getting from him that he had a lot of remorse and regret about committing suicide. I was getting that "the voices made him do it." I asked her if there was any more information on his death and if he possibly had some mental health issues where he heard voices, and guess what? She said, "*Yes!*"

Was I feeling the pain and regret he felt as a spirit after committing suicide? It's possible. This experience of "seeing" spirits was not terrifying like the spirit at the Buchanan though. This was more of a sad feeling. I wanted to help him so he didn't have to feel this pain. I don't know what his crime had been or why he was in there, but I didn't care about that. He was so sad and so regretful; I wanted to help him feel peace. He does not like talking about what he did to himself. He really does not like talking at all. He likes to be left alone. So we respected that and did not try to communicate with him any longer.

As the investigation went on, I was also "seeing" an old inmate of the jail. This guy was more from your 50s era. He was in a black and white jump suit, had greased dark black hair, and had a menacing smile. He lied up on top of the jail cells and just looked down at us like we were nothing. It was just Sarah, Hannah and I in there at that time. It was almost as if he thought he was superior to us. He didn't really say much, just laughed a lot. He didn't stick around for very long either. After he left, I "saw" something a lot more disturbing and sad.

All of the sudden, I started "seeing" a little girl. She was burnt by a fire. Her hair was frail and thin, and half of her face had been burnt. She was wearing a white dress that also had black char on it from the fire. She looked at me and was very timid.

There was also a little boy with her in overalls. He did not have any burn marks on him, but he resembled the girl quite a bit, as if they were brother and sister.

I did not try to communicate with her directly, instead, I asked the tour guide if there had been a fire nearby and if there had been any casualties. She was unsure, but her friend that was with us knew the town history well. She said, yes, there had been a fire in the early 1900s and the family that lived there died, including two children.

I, honestly, can't even describe my emotions when she told me that. This was probably the best "vision" I had had since the Buchanan County Home. However, this "sighting" was much different. I couldn't feel much of the little girl's emotions. She was just there, looking, and was more curious than anything about who we were and what we were doing.

We did actually catch some EVPs that are of children laughing and one child crying. Could this be the two children I saw? We will be heading back for more answers in the future.

As the night progressed, activity ceased. It was just like a switch flipped off and the spirits went quiet. It was only around 12:30 AM, so it was still really early in the world of investigating. We decided to pack up and go home and let them rest.

In my opinion, since this was something new for them, it tired them out really quickly. I describe spirit energy manifestation to people as though it's like they are running a mile just to say, "Hi," in the audio recorder. Is this the case for all spirits? No. Some have the energy of a Tesla Coil, but most that we encounter have to find a large energy source to interact with us. Your body is the main source of energy for spirits, especially in a location that does not have a lot of electricity. If you've ever heard of a "paranormal hangover," that is why. It is the spirit taking your energy to use it to communicate and interact with you.

EDINBURGH at BOBBY MacKEY'S

It was early September 2013, when Josh, our friend and I decided to take the road trip down to Lexington, Kentucky to attend ScareFest. This is about an eight hour drive for us. We got up bright and early and left at 4:00 AM so we could make it down for the first day of the convention.

ScareFest is a convention in which many people come together to see some of the most highlighted paranormal celebrities, movie celebrities, and representatives of some of the most haunted locations in America. I was so excited to see Grant Wilson, Steve Gonsalves and Dave Tango from *Ghost Hunters*. I had watched *Ghost Hunters* since it started!

Well, we finally had made it down to Lexington, and what did we do? We took a really long, needed nap. However, we still made it to the convention with plenty of time to get our first day excitement jitters out.

You may be wondering, why am I telling a story about a convention? Remember, I am a paranormal investigator, and we take any opportunity to investigate a haunted location when we can, especially those that aren't in Iowa! However, we didn't realize we would be doing a small investigation until we were on our way back home.

The first night in Kentucky we decided to head out to "Wicked World Haunted Attraction." So, we got a good scare from a commercial haunt while we were down. I honestly think the grounds of Wicked World could be haunted. If you think of all of the history that could have taken place there, it is bound to have a good ghost story. However, this is not where my ghost story begins. Like I said, it begins when the vacation came to an end.

We were on our way home, and we had to drive through Cincinnati, Ohio. Our friend that was with us mentioned, "Bobby Mackey's is near Cincinnati."

Saying something like this to a paranormal investigator makes your internal navigation system turn on and direct you towards the haunted location. Okay, we still had to use GPS, but you get what I'm saying. We are drawn to these places, and we *have* to go see them if we are that close to them.

We quickly typed in "Bobby Mackey's Music World" in our GPS and there we were, off to Bobby Mackey's. I, honestly, didn't know the entire history to the haunting there, and was informed about it on our drive there by our friend who was with us. Apparently, it is said that there is a portal to hell within Bobby Mackey's. There are many legends as to why Bobby Mackey's is haunted, and the most commonly told is about two men who murdered a pregnant woman, cut off her head and placed it over the drains. This is said to have been a Satanic Ritual. Many years later, it is said that the old caretaker uncovered the old well and there the portal to hell was opened. This not only opened the portal, but the caretaker also became possessed.

The other story is your typical love story. In the 1940s, one of the performers at the performance hall fell in love with a man her father didn't approve. Mobsters killed her lover, she drank poison and she died. She wrote of her love in a diary which is said to have been found by the caretaker when he was uncovering the well, and boom, he became possessed. This story is much more "shaky" than the other and really has no large relation to the current building, but you will find this story in many of the haunted history books.

So, let's get to the point of this story and why I am telling it. The minute we pulled into the Bobby Mackey's parking lot, we felt the rush of negative, dark, heavy energy. It was an "all eyes on us" type of situation. We decided to hook up the ghost box to the car, so we could hear it nice and clear. We started asking questions.

We asked, "What is in this building?"

We got "devil," "demon" and "evil." That makes sense, according to what they say is in the building. I, honestly, don't think I would ever step foot in that building. It screams evil when you look at it.

The title of this section is *Edinburgh at Bobby Mackey's* and here's why. While conducting the ghost box session, our friend asked, "What is your purpose here?"

Across the ghost box we heard, "Edinburgh,"

What?

Remember how I told you we have a certain someone who likes to follow us to other haunted locations? Well I am 99.9% sure he followed us on down to Kentucky just to visit Bobby Mackey's with us.

We asked, "Is this the Joker?" and we heard, "Yes."

We couldn't believe it. This was the first time we had him come across the ghost box with us not being at Edinburgh Manor. This is when we found out that he could follow us from haunted location to haunted location.

I will say, I have never felt him in our home, and if I ever did, you better believe I would be cleansing in a heartbeat.

We were all taken aback a little bit by this response, because we didn't think we'd be getting a place that's hundreds of miles away come across the ghost box, let alone, the "Joker!" We took advantage of this situation to ask some more questions, but he just messed with us. He kept saying "demon" and "devil" anytime we asked a question.

We had gotten enough, so we put the ghost box away, got out of the car and walked around the parking lot and grounds to get a feel of the energy. We then took a few pictures, got back in the car and continued on with our drive home.

I mention this story in this book because I want people to understand there are some spirits that can follow you and do not stay in one location. This is why it is so important to research this field and how to protect and ground yourself. You may research a location and understand what you're looking for, but you also need to know what to do if you find what you're looking for.

THE HAUNTED HOUSE ON THE HILLTOP

There is a private residence home in Cedar Rapids that dates back to 1876 that sits on a hilltop off First Avenue. The home before 2013 was an eye sore since it sat there vacant for many years. In 2013, a local Cedar Rapidian purchased the home and restored it back to its full potential and beauty.

He was friends with a close friend of mine and had been telling her all about the ghosts that had been making themselves known during the restoration. She found this to be the perfect opportunity to reach out to me and ask if we'd be willing to investigate. The only stipulation was she had to be there.

This really wasn't a stipulation to Josh or I. It was more of an incentive for us to really want to investigate this home. We knew she would be hilarious and potentially spark up more activity since she was a first-time investigator. Josh and I had already been gawking over this home since it was so close to our own home, and we could just feel the haunting oozing from the exterior of the house. On top of that, there is a funeral home right across the street.

The owner of the home was in California at the time but trusted our friend, Josh and I enough to let us in the home while he was gone. We got the key from his mother who lives right behind the house in her own home, and went in to soak up the house we couldn't wait to get into.

The owner had sent me some stories about what had been going on in the home. There was a contractor in the house with him one time and the owner did not like the work he was doing. He voiced his concerns to the contractor and he continued on to tell me that the contractor had an attitude with him. The contractor had to go out to his truck to get a few things, and when he got to the stairs which are right inside the side door, he took a step down and felt something push him from behind. He flew down the stairs! Fortunately, he wasn't hurt, but he told the owner he felt two hands push him down the stairs.

The owner's theory on this is that the spirits are protective of him and when they saw this contractor giving him grief they didn't like it. He has never felt threatened by the spirits, but protected by them. I asked him if he thought they would care if we were coming in trying to seek them and communicate with them. He said he had already told them we were coming and that they shouldn't be alarmed or scared.

We got to the house in the evening of the investigation, we setup a few audio recorders, and cameras, and began in the upstairs parlor. In the parlor there is a wood stove, an old sewing machine, and a few chairs. Then off to the left of the top of the stairs is the master bedroom. I sat near the wood stove, Josh was walking around and our friend was sitting in front of me. We heard some bangs from the main floor and also from the master bedroom. These are not your house shifting types of bangs; these were bangs on the wall, and they were loud.

We conducted an EVP blast session in the parlor area. We could just feel all of the eyes watching us in the home. They were curious about us even though they were told we were okay to be in the home. We listened back to the audio recorder after about a minute and a half of recording. We ended up catching a voice and a sound that was almost like a cat meowing. The voice, however, we would have to really decipher what they were meaning. The voice said, "I see you," paused for about two seconds, then said, "Let me out."

One of the biggest frustrations in this field is trying to figure out what the spirits mean by some of the things they say. The "I see you," could just be them saying they see us. The, "Let me out," still confuses me to this day. From what do they want let out?

Josh and I were asked to go back again to the home a few months later. I was excited to get back to the home so I could see if I could get answers to the, "Let me out," EVP. When we went back, it was almost like someone had shut off the paranormal switch. There was nothing. There were no sounds, voices, bangs, and the eyes watching us were gone, too. We decided to lie on the bed in the master bedroom to see if we would start hearing anything. To be honest, I pretty much fell asleep. There was nothing, not even the house shifting to make a noise. It was so silent in the home. Could this be that the spirits were comfortable with us and didn't feel they needed to make themselves known to us anymore? I have no clue. Lucky, Josh and I lived only a few minutes away from the house, so we didn't worry about being too tired to drive home. We stayed in the home for a few hours, and then decided we better just head home so we don't end up falling asleep in the house.

That would be the last time we would be at the Haunted House on the Hilltop. The owner is now permanently living there. I do wonder if he ever has any activity in the home or if the spirits have become so comfortable that they are at rest.

Grand Opera House

In the winter months we try to find locations that have heat. It is not fun sitting in a freezing building, and I think the spirits get "cold," too, in the winter months. I am not saying we've never had activity in the winter, but they seem to be more out and about if they can be in a warm environment.

The Grand Opera House in Dubuque, Iowa, was the perfect location for a cold night. It had heat, and it was huge! There was so much to explore in this old theater. The Grand Opera House is one of the oldest theaters that served the public before 1900. Construction began in 1889 with an investment of $100,000 to build the historic landmark. The first production was on August 14, 1890. The theater is still a working theater today, so there is a lot of energy that gets brought into the old theater on a daily basis. This, in my opinion, energizes the atmosphere for spirits to be able to communicate and manifest.

After we got a tour of the old theater, we began to setup our equipment. On the top floor of the building is the costume room. The costumes made this room extremely creepy, but better yet, it was one of their most active rooms, according to the tour guide. The biggest feeling I got in there was the feeling of being watched. It was a little unsettling up there since you didn't know what was going to come around the corner of the racks upon racks of costumes. We actually didn't spend too much time in the costume room as we would find the main theater area gave us the activity we were looking for.

In the bottom level of the theater there are what look like tunnels and other areas where props are stored. There are some really old props in the basement area. This made me wonder, what could be connected or attached to these props? The basement area also had the "creep out" factor to it with all of the props. We wouldn't spend much time down there either, again, since we found the activity to be more prominent in the main theater area that night.

The investigation started off hot. I was sitting in the front row of the seats, one of our teammates was sitting on the stage, the other in the seats way in the back and Josh was in the pit area. I got up and sat on the edge of the stage, so I was facing the back of the theater. The entryways to the theater are these beautiful archways. We were conducting an EVP blast and we kept hearing noises within the theater. Before we pushed "Play" to listen back to the audio, my teammate and I saw a shadow figure walk across the archway. They were in the area right outside of the theater, and walked very slowly across the archway. The light from the main lobby area allowed us to see this shadow so clearly. We quickly asked, "Who are you? Can you come talk to us?"

It did not come back, but we then listened to audio. Even though we weren't able to make out what it was saying, there was a very loud voice on Josh's audio recorder. During the EVP blast we had two audio recorders going. We listened back to our teammate's audio recorder, and nothing. These audio recorders weren't even three feet apart from each other and only Josh's caught the voice. It is known that spirits can make themselves known to only certain people. Was this the case during this EVP blast? That audio was enough to startle Josh though, that he quickly came up to the main theater area from the pits. He climbed his way up, too, instead of walking through all of the tunnels to get back up.

After we had the experience in the theater, we decided to see if we could catch up on anything in the costume room. We took the long elevator ride up, and it was just like a horror movie -- the elevator opened right up to all of the costumes. There's not even a room before it to prepare yourself. I freaked myself out thinking there would be something standing there as the elevator doors opened. Nothing was standing there, but the anticipation was a killer.

We walked around and got a feel for the costume room. Again, we had that creepy feeling of being watched, and we didn't know what lied around the next costume rack. The main thing I remember from the costume area was that one of the racks of costumes started to sway back and forth. I asked Josh and my other teammates if they were moving this rack, and they weren't anywhere near it.

With such a rich history and with its beautiful edifice, the Grand Opera House in Dubuque, Iowa, is the perfect place for a spirit to reside. I wonder how many performances are residual that play for the employees and those who have passed and are still there to enjoy a "night on the town."

VILLISCA AXE MURDER HOUSE

Villisca is one location that every paranormal investigator longs to investigate, even those who just want to get a taste of paranormal investigating. Or maybe they just want to have a really good adrenaline rush, because you know the minute you step foot in that house you're going to feel a rush of rage go through you.

For those who are not familiar with the Villisca Axe Murders, here is a brief overview. On June 9th, 1912, Josiah and Sarah Moore, along with their children, Katherine, Herman, Boyd and Paul went to the local church service. Also attending that service was Ina and Lena Stillinger. They lived just outside of Villisca on the Stillinger Farm. After the service Ina and Lena went home with the Moore's since Katherine had invited them over for a sleepover.

The murderer entered the Moore's home and stayed in the attic until he committed the murders.

In the early morning on June 10, 1912, the Moore's neighbor, Mary Peckham, noticed that the Moore's home was quite still for being 7:00 AM. She went over and let out their chickens, knocked on the door, and even tried to go in, but it was locked. She then called upon Josiah's brother, Ross Moore, to come check it out. He entered the house and went into the room where Ina and Lena Stillinger were. He noted in his testimony that he did not stay long in the house to investigate further after seeing the blood-soaked sheets. He went outside and told Mrs. Peckham to call the Marshal.

There were multiple suspects, and to this day it is still unknown who the murder was. The suspects were Frank Jones, William "Blackie" Mansfield, Reverend George Jacklin Kelly, Henry Lee Moore, Andy Sawyer, and Joe Ricks. Frank Jones and Reverend George Kelly would end up being the suspects that were most likely to be the murders. But again, we still do not know, to this day, who did it.

The motive for Jones was that Josiah had worked for him and ended up leaving to manage part of the John Deere Franchise. It is also said that he Josiah had an affair with Jones' daughter-in-law.

Reverend Kelly is another story. You look at pictures of this guy and your skin crawls. What his motive was, no one knows. He said that the "voices" made him do it and he saw a black mass outside of the Moore's house that pointed and said, "Slay, utterly."

Kelly was arrested and tried for the murders. His first trial was a hung jury, and he was acquitted in the second trial. You can read much more about these murders online. This is still the number one unsolved murder case in Iowa, if not America.

My first investigation of the Villisca Axe Murder house was in August 2013. I was supposed to go that July with a different team but ended up not being a part of that team anymore when the time came. Josh knew that I was really looking forward to that investigation, so he told me that he would go with me whenever I wanted. How amazing he is! Josh and I geared up for the four-hour drive, and met a friend there. It was only the three of us there to investigate. We were told by the tour guide that we had some "big balls" to be staying in this house with just the three of us. Low and behold, it would end up being pretty much just Josh and I for a majority of the night.

I want to first describe the atmosphere of the house. When you walk into the kitchen door, you feel a huge burst of energy hit you. It is a mixture of sadness, hatred, rage, curiosity, and so much more. You first want to know, why… why were these innocent people bludgeoned to death in their sleep? Then you walk through the home and, again, feel a mix of emotions.

When you first walk in and you're in the kitchen, if you walk straight you'll find yourself in the living room, or parlor, area. Once you go through the threshold of the kitchen to the parlor, to the right is the room Ina and Lena were in. This is also known as the "Blue Room", due to the blue walls. This room, to me, has the feeling of struggle. It's thought that Lena may have been one of the only ones to put up a fight and see the face of her killer due to the position of her body when she was found. The agony and pain you feel in this room is greater for some reason than in any other room. When you go up the stairs, which are in the kitchen, it leads right into Josiah and Sarah's room. There is still a gouge in the wall from the axe hitting the wall when the killer was swinging.

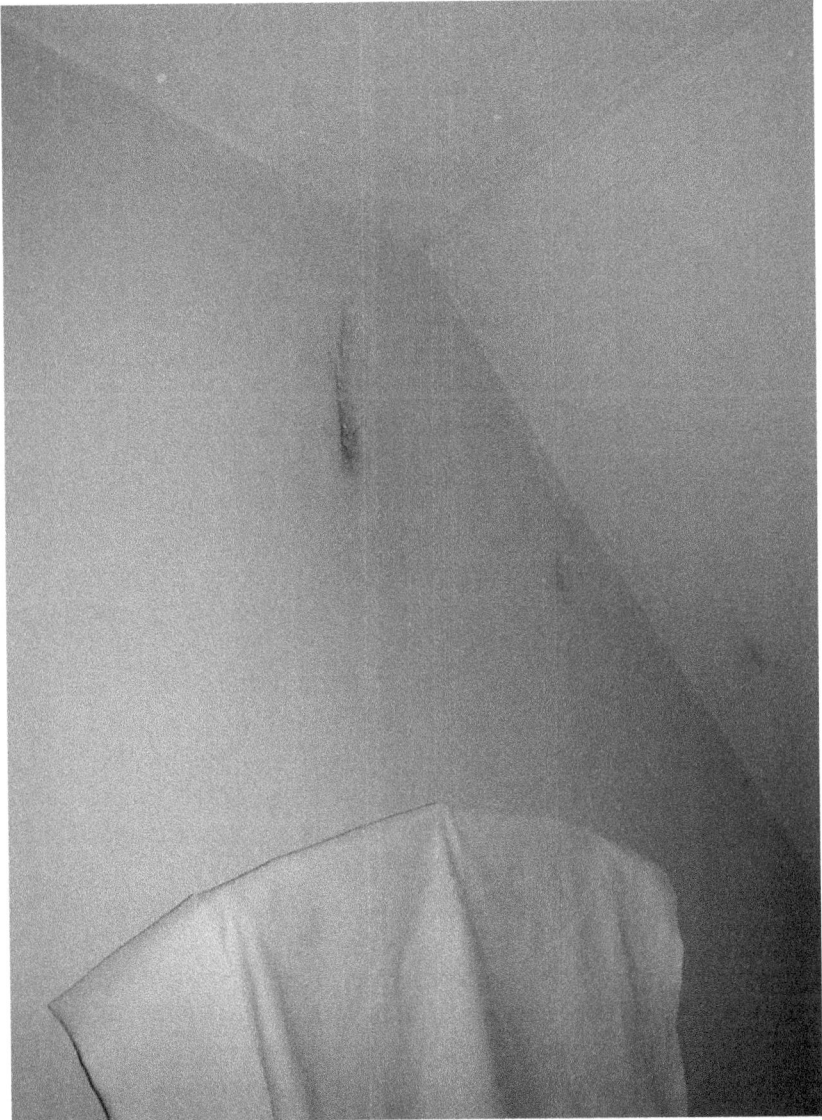

This is so eerie to look upon. You can feel the hatred from the killer by just looking at this gouge. This house is so small, but it has so much energy.

You walk through a small corridor and you are immediately in the children's room. The attic door is off of Josiah and Sarah's room, in the corridor area. There are toys and other objects left behind from previous investigators to use as trigger objects. I do not use those objects while investigating here. One, I hope and pray the family is no longer there, since they should not have to be reliving that tragic night in the afterlife. And two, since I don't believe it's the family and children there, the trigger objects really may have nothing to trigger. I really do not think the family, Ina and Lena, nor the killer are there. I think whatever is in this house has been brought in by the thousands, if not millions, of people who have now visited this home.

Another little important piece of information, it has been suspected that a well-known heavy metal band performed a Satanic Ritual in the cellar area. I refuse to go in the cellar.

The sun started to go down and we were ready to start investigating. The first investigation there started off with a bang. Literally. There were bangs here and there, and we sat in the parlor just listening to them. We decided to turn on the ghost box, and we weren't even asking any questions when the word "demon" came over it.

This shook our friend up pretty bad, and that is when he called it a night. He packed up and left, and it was just Josh and I to fend for ourselves.

When we were told we had to have some "pretty big balls" to be in there by ourselves, and that was an understatement. I don't think Josh and I were ready for what came next.

We did take a break when our friend left and collect ourselves to gear up for our next round.

We went into the house, and we wanted to go upstairs, but we couldn't. There was a presence that was so heavy that it kept us from moving. We were lucky that we made it into the parlor. We sat down to get as comfortable as we could get (if comfortable was even possible), and we started to conduct an EVP session. We thought the night was starting to die down when it was about 1:45 AM. I was shocked we lasted that long since our friend left probably around 8:00 PM.

We were just about to get up and leave when, all of the sudden, we smelled something absolutely rancid. It smelled like sulfuric acid, and it burned our noses. It was so vile. We immediately looked at each other, said, "Nope!" and ran out of the house.

We know what vile smells can mean, and this would have been the place to lure in such activity with all of the negativity and vulnerability that goes through that house on a day-to-day basis.

We got out to the barn where we kept out belongings, and we could still smell it. The odd thing was, we couldn't actually smell it outside. We quickly grabbed our gear, threw it in the car, and once we got off property, said our words of protection, and left.

I thought this would be my only and last visit to the Villisca Axe Murder House. I am not sure why I would even want to go back given the activity we had just experienced. However, I found myself back there in November 2015, with my lovely team, Unknown Darkness.

This time at the Villisca Axe Murder House, I was now aware of my way to "see" spirit. I must have really had my guard up, though, because I did not have any visions, but I could feel them.

Ina and Lena's room, again, was the strongest. The closet in that room also felt like a small child was hiding in it. As I mentioned earlier, I do not think, and also hope, that the victims are not there. I think I also could have been sensing a childlike figure, but was it actually a child? Or was it something that wanted me to think it was a child to lure me into the closet and get closer? I didn't want to find out. I did not go in the closet.

We made our way up to the bedrooms upstairs, only to find this extremely scary clown doll that Shannon would torture us with the entire day and night. That was probably the scariest part of this investigation.

Our second investigation turned out to be fairly quiet until we went back and reviewed evidence. That is the wonderful thing about this field; you may not have personal experiences, but evidence review may uncover so many things!

I also want to mention we were at Villisca when the day tours were not going. They are only run during the spring and summer months. Also, knowing the man who lives in Mary Peckham's house and is the tour guide at the home, he let us in quite early!

We got to the house about 10:00 AM, we setup our DVR cameras and audio recorders, and we left. We do this pretty often, actually. So, if we catch a shadow or anything moving on camera while we're gone, we know it wasn't us. Audio is a little tougher, however, since there could be voices and sounds caught from outside. There are some voices we can tell are not outside voices, but one has to be careful with claiming something is paranormal in those circumstances.

A few weeks after the investigation, I got a text message from Shannon asking if Josh and I could come over to watch the DVR footage from Villisca. Of course, we did since we really enjoy hanging out with Shannon and Sarah outside of the paranormal field, as well. This was a great opportunity to enjoy their company and also watch the footage.

The first video was from Ina and Lena's room. He told us to watch the dresser on the lower part of the screen. We were watching and, all of the sudden, a very short and fast shadow appeared. It looked as though it came through the door of the bedroom and ran toward the wall where the window is. If this would have been one of us (which it definitely wasn't since we are not transparent), we would have hurt ourselves running into the wall. This figure was so short and it moved so quickly. To this day, we still are in shock when we watch that piece of evidence, and we show it to people who come to our presentations.

This was not the only shadow figure we caught at Villisca, however. Shannon continued after that video piece and said, "Well, there's more."

He then got the DVR set to the correct time to watch the next video clip. This clip was in the kitchen. We had the DVR camera setup right next to the oven on the left side to face the parlor entryway and the stairs. In the first part of this video the camera moves, as though something grabbed it and shifted it to the right and downward. Then, all of the sudden, the camera jumped an hour ahead and a shadow could be seen moving from the kitchen door to the parlor entryway. We thought the shadow was unbelievable, but how in the world do you explain the time jumping an hour ahead? The timestamp shifted immediate from 13:00 and some minutes to 14:00 and some minutes.

Our theory is whatever was in the kitchen at that time manipulated it. Do we know why? No, we do not. This is still a mystery to us, and it probably always will be.

We also caught some EVPs that night of children's voices and, also, a low gravely growl.

Well, I said I was done with Villisca, but this investigation left open too many unanswered questions. I'm sure our team will plan to go back in the near future.

KATIE HOPKINS

GHOST HUNTING 101 BECOMING A PARANORMAL INVESTIGATOR

Many people ask me, "Katie, how did you become a paranormal investigator?"

The main thing I tell them is, "I got involved and participated in local events."

I could have stopped after the Russell House back in February 2012, but it didn't feel right to stop. I researched and looked for events to attend. That is how I found the first team I was on, 319 Paranormal.

In this chapter I am going to highlight the four most important aspects of becoming a paranormal investigator. These include participating and attending events, researching the paranormal, being open (but not too open), and having fun!

The first part of attending events is very important. This is the networking part of becoming a paranormal investigator. This allows you to see many different approaches and styles of investigating. There may be some styles you agree with and some you don't. This helps shape you as an investigator. You can use the tools you learn from others and even modify them to your liking and your style. This also allows you to gain experience investigating with experienced investigators. With that being said, do your research on the team holding the event too. You want to make sure they are credible, and you want to make sure you agree with their approach to investigating.

My first investigation was with a team whom I knew. I knew them personally, so I also knew their personalities. I trusted them and knew I was safe and comfortable with their investigation style.

HARRIS HAVEN FUNERAL HOME HAUNTED HOUSE

SOLD OUT

Unknown Darkness

JUNE 11TH, 2016

8:00PM-2:00AM

The second part, researching the paranormal field, is probably one of the most important steps to becoming a paranormal investigator. When I say research the paranormal, I don't mean research the locations you are investigating. Yet, this is also a very important step as a paranormal investigator. I want to focus on researching the actual field of the paranormal, though.

It is very important to know what a ghost means, what types of hauntings you can encounter, and how to handle them. It is also important to know the traits of an empath. We will cover all of these in the next chapter. For now, I just want to give you the basics of things you should know about becoming an investigator.

The next step I mention is being open (but not too open). Do not claim everything is paranormal, look for things that are possibly not paranormal. This is called debunking. Debunking means trying to find a natural cause for the activity that is being claimed.

For example, someone claims that their kitchen door slammed shut. A good idea would be to look for any types of drafts that could cause the door to slam. Were windows open at the time? Search for any elements that could have possibly caused the door to slam shut. If it cannot be explained, then it may be paranormal. The phrase we hold strong to is, "When in doubt, throw it out."

The last step is have fun! You must have fun when investigating. I don't mean running around and screwing around during an investigation, but have a little bit of a sense of humor, and enjoy your time with your team. There are times when you are going to get bored and you're going to get tired because there may not be much activity going on at the location. Do not let this discourage you. Have fun with your team. Sometimes when spirits see you are having fun, that's when they want to come out and play.

KATIE HOPKINS

WHAT IS PARANORMAL?

This is where we will delve deeper into what a spirit is and what types of hauntings you may come across during a paranormal investigation. There are four main types of hauntings, including: intelligent, residual, poltergeist and demonic. I will also explain signs of being an empath and being able to sense spirit. This is what I consider myself to be when I say I sense spirit and also visualize them.

Let's start off with what a spirit is and who is most likely to become a spirit. A ghost (spirit or apparition) is the energy, soul or personality of a person who has died and is stuck between our realm of existence and the next (has not crossed over). A ghost can be perceived by the living in a number of ways: through sight (apparitions), sound (voices), smell (fragrances and odors), touch, and sometimes can be sensed.

An example of "touch" is being scratched. Josh was scratched at Edinburgh Manor right below the cross on his arm. This was a way for the spirit to communicate or make itself known. It wasn't necessarily harming Josh, but this could possibly have been the only way he or she was able to express their presence.

Now that I have told you what a spirit is, who becomes a spirit? Not everyone becomes a spirit in their afterlife. Those most likely to become a spirit are those who have many unfulfilled desires. This is typically those who have passed on traumatically and have not completed everything in the physical world that they had wanted.

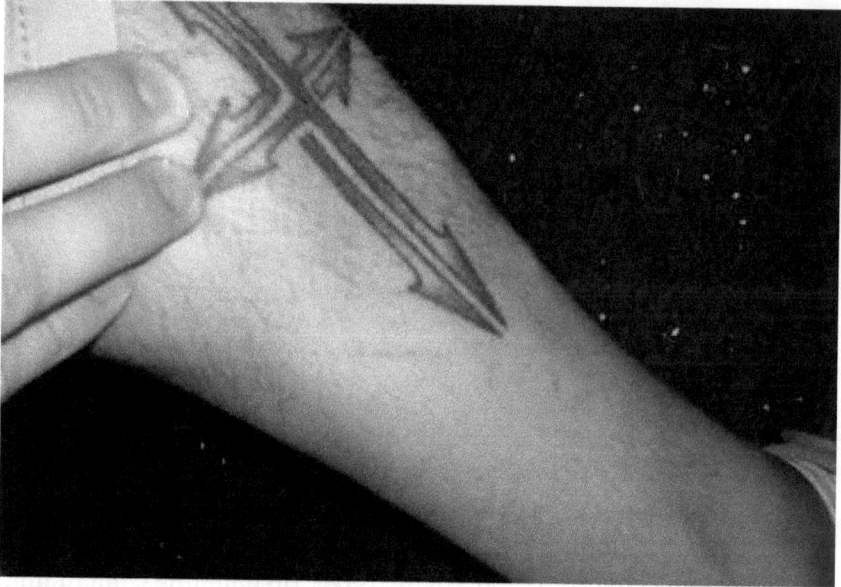

The next trait of those who are most likely to become a spirit are people with personality defects, such as anger, fear, greed, high amount of ego, etc. The characteristic that sticks out to me is "high amount of ego." This makes me think this person who has become a spirit feels they are too good to leave the physical world. The word that comes to mind is narcissist.

The next characteristic of those who are more likely to become a spirit is lack of spiritual practice. The reason for this would be that this person does not have a progressive level of surrender of their mind, body and intellect. It blocks them from crossing over. They lack spiritual practice consisting of progressive level of surrender of mind, body and intellect.

The last one, and probably one of the most well-known characteristics, is unfinished business. This is when a living person who passes away has business in the physical world that they were not able to complete while living. This could be such things as getting married or traveling to a certain location. The one thing that comes to mind is they weren't able to finish their bucket list.

Types of Hauntings

First, you must know, what are the signs of a haunting? These include unexplained noises, unexplained shadows, change in energy (around you and your own energy), strange animal behavior, and feelings of being watched. What I want to make sure everyone understands, if your dog or cat starts acting up for some odd reason, does this automatically mean your house is haunted? No. It is a combination of all of the traits listed that could lead you to believe your house is haunted. If you are experiencing any of these, it would be wise to consult someone who is knowledgeable in the paranormal field.

You also want to be careful just calling out, "Is someone here?" or "Who is here?" This is like an invitation for paranormal activity. It gives the spirit the "okay" to make themselves known or invite themselves into your home. My biggest advice is if you are experiencing any of these characteristics, and especially if you're experiencing more than one, consult someone who you trust in the paranormal field. If you do not know anyone, research local paranormal teams.

The first type of haunting, which is one of the most common, is an intelligent haunting. This is a spirit who tries to interact with the living. There are times that the sprits might not know they have passed, and others might be aware of it and have come to convey a message to someone. Intelligent spirits are often the result of a spirit needing some sort of help and wants you to help them. There are many signs of an intelligent haunting, and they can include hearing voices and seeing an apparition.

The next type and another very common haunting is a residual haunting. I touched base on residual hauntings in the Snowden House chapter. A residual haunting is just like a record player. It is a moment in time in history that is being replayed in the present time. They are similar to a recorded tape; the events will be played time and again. They are always repeating. The most common reasons for a residual haunting are when a traumatic event happens, negative or positive energy is created and leaves behind an imprint of a particular event. The entities involved in a residual haunting are not aware of their surroundings.

A poltergeist haunting can often be confused with a demonic haunting. This is why it is important to research types of hauntings and know the characteristics of them. This is a fairly popular type of haunting in which the spirit or poltergeist, at times, is malevolent. A poltergeist makes its presence felt by moving objects, creating noises and assaulting animals and people. Poltergeist activities include throwing or moving of objects or pieces of furniture, vile smells, shrieks and loud noises. Poltergeists can also cause a disturbance in telephones and various other electronic equipment. They can also turn appliances and lights on and off and can hit, bite, and attack a person. Activity from a poltergeist can start and stop suddenly. Its duration can last for seconds, minutes, hours, months and even years.

The last, and most controversial haunting, is a demonic haunting. These are the most uncommon hauntings and, most likely, you will never come across one. Many people get poltergeist and elemental hauntings confused with demonic hauntings. The reason for that is because a poltergeist and elemental can mimic the characteristics of a demonic haunting, but they aren't nearly as strong.

Here are some important pieces of information and signs of a demonic haunting to keep in mind. A demon never had any human form, and their main purpose is to create chaos and destruction and cause stress or even death. This next piece of information is extremely important. A demon possesses people, not objects. It manipulates objects to open up the "targeted" person. For example, it will move a doll, and make it seem like a friendly spirit to get your approval and attention. Once a person opens up, that is when the chaos beings.

There are three stages of a demonic haunting that lead to possession: Infestation, Oppression and Possession. Infestation is when objects in the house are moving and being manipulated. This is when the demon is gaining your trust. Oppression is when the demon makes its identity known and moves into "attack" mode. This stage is designed to "break" the target and get them to give-in to the demon. The final stage is possession. The demon has possessed the target and is in full control of them. There are many signs of a demonic haunting. The most well-known include vile smells, scratches (usually three marks mocking the Holy Trinity), knocking in "threes," and crucifixes turned upside down on their own.

I have never witnessed a demonic haunting and hope and pray I never do. Even with the knowledge of how to identify it, it is a haunting that is so strong you may not have the tools to get rid of it.

Signs of an Empath

Throughout this book you have been able to read about the empathic experiences I have had. There are signs to understand if you have empathic abilities. The one thing I will point out though is, we *all* have empathic abilities. Being an empath is merely the ability to sense another person's energy. This could be the energy of a living person or a deceased person.

Some of the characteristics of an empath are feeling other emotions, negativity is overwhelming to you, you have a strong intuition, and you can feel symptoms of those around you. You can, also, experience a high amount of fatigue. The reason I say that we all have empathic abilities is because everyone has an intuition. There are some people that may have a higher sense of empathic feelings than others. These are the people who are able to sense spirits around them, and in my case, visualize them from time-to-time.

KATIE HOPKINS

HISTORY OF THE PARANORMAL

It just wouldn't be a "Katie Hopkins" book without the history of the paranormal within the book. I have done much research on the history of the paranormal, and if really if you wanted to date it back before the United States, you could go all the way back to 1692 in Salem, Massachusetts, during the Salem Witch Trials. However, I'm more of a Victorian Era Historian, and I have researched the paranormal during the height of the Spiritualist Movement in the United States and the United Kingdom.

The height of the Spiritualist Movement in the United States and the United Kingdom began in 1848 with the Fox sisters. The Fox sisters consist of Maggie (Margaret), Kate (Katherine) and Leah Fox.

They are remembered for their raps and taps code to communicate with spirits to which they were credited for about 37 years. They were said to be able to communicate by having spirits tap a code to them. They could tap "yes" or "no" with a certain number of taps (usually one for yes and two for no). They could also tap the alphabet by tapping so many times to a certain letter. For example, the letter "C" would be three taps. This was the spirit's way of spelling out a message to them.

The sisters traveled all over to perform their communication methods with the spirits. This eventually lead to the fall of the Fox sisters. They all succumbed to alcoholism which eventually led to the discredit of their communication with spirits. In 1885, spiritualism was starting to dwindle. Many were starting to investigate fraudulent practices of mediumship and communication with spirits. This also was a time of tragedy for the Fox sisters as Kate's husband had died right in front of them. Adding to the demise, again, was alcohol. Maggie was called into a counsel to prove her communication skills and it failed miserably. All of the sisters died within three years of each other in the early 1890s. Many blame their timely deaths on their fame and fall.

The United Kingdom was also a very prominent place during the Spiritualist movement. Queen Victoria was known for holing a séance or two. In 1861, her beloved Prince Albert died at Windsor Castle, leaving her a widow, and she never fully recovered from her depression. She found the one thing to bring her a peace of mind was to have séances to speak with her passed lover.

Queen Victoria hired thirteen-year-old Robert James Lees to perform séances for her in Windsor Castle. At one of the séances, the thirteen-year-old surprised the Queen with his talents and called her by a name that only she would know. It was said that

Prince Albert would speak through Lees and have conversations with the Queen. During one of the séances Lees called the Queen by her pet name that only Prince Albert and the Queen knew. This was validation for the Queen that Prince Albert was there and that he was with her in another realm.

History, Use and Danger of Ouija Boards

This book wouldn't be complete without tapping on the history and use of Ouija Boards. Ouija Boards were very different back during the Spiritualist Movement than what we are accustomed to today. The use of the Ouija Board began in the United States in 1840s to connect with the spirit world. These sessions were usually led by mediums who claimed to be intermediaries between the living and the dead.

The creation of the board started off by using a table and the board was created on the floor. The table would move to letters on the board (floor), spelling out a message to those who were conducting the session. It had "Yes," "No," and "Goodbye" like the modern-day boards you see. You also only needed one other person to "run" the board.

The modern Ouija Board became popular in 1890s. It was created by Elijah Bond, Charles Kennard and William H.A. Maupin. Later on in the Twentieth Century, the board would be picked up by popular toy companies like Hasbro, bringing much controversary to many homes with children who would sneak away to play the Ouija Board.

I'll be honest. I played with a Ouija Board when I was younger. It was nothing but a way to get a good cheap thrill in my parents' and neighbor's basements. Also, being the youngest of four children, I had to do what my siblings wanted to do. They enjoyed scaring me with such things like the Ouija Board. I remember playing with one as a kid with my siblings, and I'm pretty sure my siblings "manipulated" it to just scare me so I would go away. We didn't know the dangers of what we were doing.

Many in the paranormal field tell you to stay away from Ouija Boards. I was one of these people right off the bat, and I still won't play with one, but I understand the board more now after doing some research.

In this field, you open yourself up to vulnerability and, sometimes, even danger depending on how you conduct investigations. The one thing I can tell you and be confident about is it is all about your methods of communication. The Ouija Board itself is not dangerous; it's the act of communication and the communication methods you are using. You are welcoming in spirits or even something worse. Those who use Ouija Boards are usually not knowledgeable on safe communication methods, therefore, they make themselves vulnerable to spirits. You never know with whom you are speaking.

Josh always said the ghost box is just an "electronic" Ouija Board. I never agreed with him on this until I researched the Ouija Board and found that it's not the board, it's the act of communication. We take many protective measures on investigations, and we, honestly, rarely use the ghost box anymore. But, this opened my eyes. Have I just been lucky over the years to not drag anything out that was unwanted?

This section isn't to tell you to go out and buy a Ouija Board and just be careful. It is to inform you about the danger of communication methods that can be used in the paranormal field. There are many people that still swear by using Ouija Boards for communication, but they are also knowledgeable about communication methods. If you are ever to use one, please be aware of the danger of your communication and to what you are "calling out." Be sure to have a specific spirit in mind with whom you wish to speak. Do not just call upon any spirit or entity. That is when you could potentially come upon an unwanted visitor.

FINAL THOUGHTS

When I sat down to write this book, I thought, oh I'll get about 50 pages and be done, I'm sure. I didn't know how to write a book, and I didn't know what to write. However, with inspiration from my good friend Adam Tillery, writing the story for the *Encounters With The Paranormal: Volume 3* book, with great support from Mike Ricksecker, and after reading Vanessa Hogle's book *Walking With Ghosts*, The main thing I had to do to get this written, was not hold back. I couldn't let fear of what others thought hold me back from writing.

Let me tell you, this has been the most liberating and enjoyable experience ever. I am so happy to put my experiences down on paper for those to read and take them as they will. I hope that this book helps others feel the urge to express their experiences, and share them with others. I was so excited to reminisce about these experiences even though some of them weren't so enjoyable at the time. But these experiences are what have made me the investigator I am today. They have opened me up to a whole new view of the paranormal.

Please, if you take anything from this book, take that it's okay to be different. It's okay to open up to something that is not considered "normal." You may be surprised what you discover. You may find the "real" you, you may find you are able to help others (both living and passed), and also, you may find the best things in life. Like your spouse.

Below are pictures of my wonderful team Unknown Darkness. I must thank them for their wonderful support and dedication to this crazy hobby of ours.

KATIE HOPKINS

ABOUT THE AUTHOR

Katie Hopkins is an avid paranormal enthusiast and historian. She graduated with her Bachelor of Arts Degree in History (specialization in Civil War History) in 2010 from the University of Northern Iowa. She also has her Master of Science in Higher Education from Kaplan University. She has been involved in the paranormal field since February 2012, but has always been intrigued by it ever since she was a little girl. She loves to research the locations the Unknown Darkness team investigates. She has been to many haunted locations in the United States to investigate, the farthest being Old South Pittsburg Hospital in Chattanooga, Tennessee. She plans to continue her research for a very long time and hopes to find the answers so many long to know about the paranormal.

Other titles from Haunted Road Media:

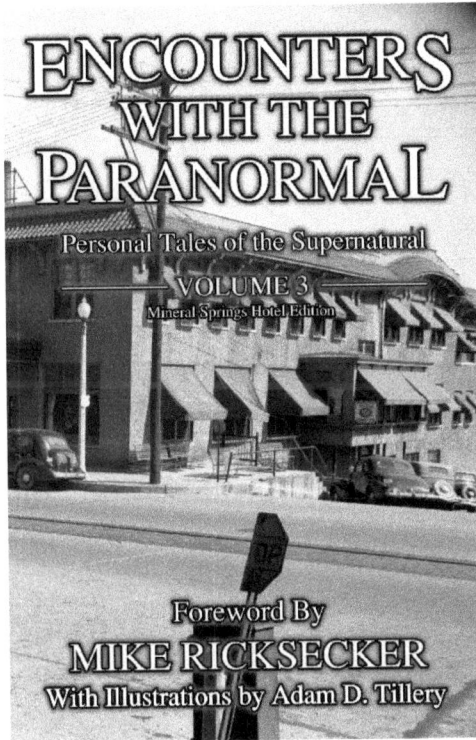

Almost everyone has a ghost story. Real people. Real stories.

In this third volume, read about more haunted houses, supernatural creatures, messages from pets from the other side, haunted history, experiences during paranormal investigations, psychic experiences, and more, including a dedicated section to the historic Mineral Springs Hotel. ENCOUNTERS WITH THE PARANORMAL: VOLUME 3 reveals more personal stories of the supernatural and paranormal, continuing to explore the realm beyond the veil through its contributors.

For more information visit:
www.hauntedroadmedia.com

www.ingramcontent.com/pod-product-compliance
Lightning Source LLC
Chambersburg PA
CBHW071028280326
41935CB00011B/1497